WORDS OF HOPE AND COMFORT

DALLAS HOLM

WORDS OF *hope* AND *comfort*

Paperback ISBN: 9781627581011

Cover and Book Design: Melody Christian, finickydesigns.com

DEDICATION

I would like to dedicate Words of Hope and Comfort to my wonderful wife, Linda. There is no one, in all my life, for whom I have greater respect and admiration.

I love you, Linda.

TABLE OF CONTENTS

INTRODUCTION

For many years, as I have read and studied God's Word, I have sought to accompany and enhance those times of study by reading devotional thoughts from other saints.

My *Utmost for His Highest* (O.Chambers), *Morning and Evening* (C.Spurgeon) and *Streams in the Desert* (C.Cowman) have been among my favorites and have each been read through many times over many years. I have often thought, "I wish I could share scriptures, stories and applications that might benefit the lives of others in ways similar to the way in which these devotionals have benefited me."

I've written many songs through the years and have released them on some thirty-eight recordings. I have been greatly blessed and encouraged by the testimonies of those who received blessing and encouragement from those songs.

It occurred to me that perhaps sharing the stories behind the songs, along with additional experiences and insights, might prove to be an extra benefit to those who have been touched by the songs I have penned.

If these stories, experiences and insights could bring glory to God and focus on His Word, then perhaps I should set myself to this task.

And so I have. *Words of Hope and Comfort* typifies the essence of the ministry God has given me through the years.

I've written many songs in numerous styles and on many topics, but always the songs designed to touch the lives of hurting people were the mainstay and center of my musical offerings.

As I wrote this devotional I occasionally shed tears, remembering some of the difficult stops along life's journey. Sometimes, as I read a chapter to my wife for her input, we would laugh so hard that, once again, tears would form.

I thought of experiences, long ago forgotten. I've shared stories never shared before.

But through it all, it has been my prayerful desire that a scripture, some line from a song or perhaps a shared experience from long ago would be a significant help and blessing to you, as you may presently need a word of hope and comfort.

There are certain themes which will be revisited throughout this book. Several references are made to Linda's battle with cancer. This has not been done to bring any undue or unnecessary attention to us or our circumstances, but rather to assure you that we too have walked the "rough roads" of life's journey and found God's grace sufficient and His faithfulness absolute.

From the rough places have come some of the polished stones. Songs birthed in "The dark night of the soul" have been some of the… *"treasures of darkness"*.

A few years ago I released the CD entitled *Songs of Hope and Comfort.* This devotional is a continuation of and an accompaniment to that project.

I hope you are able to read this devotional and also listen to the songs which inspired this book.

Most of all, I pray you receive encouragement, joy, healing and peace through these *Words of Hope and Comfort.*

HERE WE ARE

Here we are in Your presence
  Lifting holy hands to You
Here we are praising Jesus
  For the things He's brought us through.

In the mid seventies while on tour with Dallas Holm and Praise, I did a radio interview on a station in Carlinville, Ill. After some minutes of conversation and questions about the tour and the evening concert, the interviewer asked a very specific question.

He asked, "Where did music come from?" After a brief recollection of my own musical journey and experience, I reflected upon such musical influences as Elvis, Ricky Nelson, The Beatles and a host of others.

I concluded he was looking for a more substantitive and historical response. My mind stretched back through my music history and theory classes in college. I recalled studying and playing the classics given us from centuries before. Still I knew I wasn't reaching back far enough.

A humorous thought skipped through my brain "...which came first, the wheel or music?" Was someone humming or whistling while inventing the wheel? That would answer the question, but only God knows the answer!

Wait a minute, there it is.... The answer. God! He created everything and apart from Him nothing was created. *"For by Him all things were created, both in the heavens and on earth, visible and invisible...all things have been created by Him and for Him" (Colossians 1:16).*

Like that kid who always had the right answer in class, I too suddenly felt I had the right answer. I responded, "Music came from God!" The interviewer smiled – then briskly moved on to the next question. "If music came from God and has eternal implications, what is its primary purpose?" *"...By Him and for Him"* the Scripture says. It suddenly seemed clear to me that the primary purpose of music was to glorify God. This may seem crystal clear to you, but as a relatively new Christian, I'm not sure I had thought about it like this. In my zeal to tell my friends and others of the marvelous life- changing love and grace of God, I almost exclusively crafted all my songs as a testimony of my failure and God's victory. My sin, His forgiveness. "I once was lost but now I'm found, was blind but now I see." I wish I had written "Amazing Grace," but in a very real sense I was writing it and re-writing it to tell the ageless story of His undying love and limitless grace. Yet now I suddenly sensed there was something more, something new, at least for me.

I was talking to others, but I wasn't really talking to God in my songs. What would that look like? What would that sound like? What would I say?

I don't have the words
To tell You how I feel
I just don't know what I can say
I'm not worthy to speak Your holy name
Yet You tell me
You love me just the same.

From this simple interview came a whole new realm of thought and expression represented in a new song entitled, "Here We Are."

I learned in speaking to God we also speak to others. We bring them along with us. They listen in, you might say.

As people listen to you, what do they hear? As they observe your life, what do they see; or perhaps we should ask, who do they see?

As Christians, everything about us should point to Jesus. The music of our lives should join the chorus of the sweet song of redemption. Remember, as Paul states, *"...it is no longer I who live, but Christ who lives in me" (Galatians 2:20).* Herein lies the essence of effective Christian communication and expression. Herein also lies the greatest challenge to our victorious living and Christian testimony.

"It's no longer I," but we're all too aware of the ample portion of *"I"* that still resides within.

We have presented our *"bodies a living sacrifice" (Romans 12:1),* but we are continually reminded of a nature within that wars against our members.

The spirit and the flesh are not easily reconciled it seems. Paul agrees:

"I do not understand what I do. For what I want to do I do not do, but what I hate I do. And if I do what I do not want to do, I agree that the law is good. As it is, it is no longer I myself who does it, but it is sin living in me. For I know that good itself does not dwell in me, that is, in my sinful nature. For I have the desire to do what is good, but I cannot carry it out. For I do not do the good I want to do, but the evil I do not want to do—this I keep on doing. Now if I do what I do not want to do, it is no longer I who do it, but it is sin living in me that does it. So I find this law at work: Although I want to do good, evil is right there with me. For in my inner being I delight in God's law; but I see another law at work in me, waging war against the law of my mind and making me a prisoner of the law of sin at work within me. What a wretched man I am! Who will rescue me from this body that is subject to death? Thanks be to God, who delivers me through Jesus Christ our Lord! So then, I myself in my mind am a slave to God's law, but in my sinful nature a slave to the law of sin" (Romans 7:15-25).

"There is therefore, now no condemnation, for those who are in Christ Jesus. For the law of the Spirit of life in Christ Jesus has set you free from the law of sin and death" (Romans 8:1-2).

I never thought that it could be this way
  And I never thought I'd be the one
But You found me dying in my sin
  And You looked at me
With love and took me in.

Like that old song says, "Just as I am without one plea." We were dying (literally and spiritually) in our sin; but He saw us, He looked at us with love and took us in.

He saw us, He loved us and He saved us! It all comes back to Him! It always does. This is precisely why we must speak for Him, sing for Him, give to Him and die to ourselves.

I continue to write songs of testimony – in fact I've written all kinds of songs in all kinds of styles to talk about all kinds of things.

Our lives are lived out in many stages through many seasons. God can and does use all these things for His glory.

Perhaps you are in a difficult season just now, being tested and tried by the realities of life in a fallen world and a corruptible body.

Maybe, as Job, you've sought help and advice from friends and family only to be disappointed by their inability to truly comfort.

Oswald Chambers says, "Prayer is not so much about getting something from God as it is just getting God."

There are times when we think if we could just get an explanation, a sound word of advice or a sense of specific direction, we would be OK.

I think, however, there are times when we just need God. No advice, explanation or plan will suffice. Things, whatever they might be, even from His hand, are not all we need. All we need is Him and Him alone.

A brief assessment of the journey of our lives through all the ups and downs, all the stresses and strains, all the joys and heartaches, will yet testify to the fact that His grace is sufficient and He is always faithful.

Let me encourage you this moment to step into His presence, just as you are, and consider the words of a simple song given to me by Him at a crucial time in my life, many years ago.

Here we are in Your Presence
   Lifting holy hands to You
Here we are praising Jesus
   For the things He's brought us through.

"I will bless the Lord at all times; His praise shall continually be in my mouth...O magnify the Lord with me, And let us exalt His name together" (Psalm 34:1, 3).

I'VE NEVER SEEN THE RIGHTEOUS FORSAKEN

I've often been asked through the years where the songs I write come from. It's not as easy a question to answer as one might think. I do believe behind each song is the moving of God by His Holy Spirit. However, I seldom say, "God gave me this song."

I believe God does give to each of us gifts and abilities. When we use these gifts and abilities for God's glory and by the inspiration of His Spirit we have a great opportunity to please His heart and bless others.

God stirs up a gifting he has given us through a multitude of means. A scripture, a scene, an experience or a comment can all be the means by which my gifting is stirred to create a song.

Sometimes songs come fast, sometimes slow. Sometimes lyrics first, other times the music.

"Rise Again" came in about ten to fifteen minutes. "I've Never Seen The Righteous Forsaken" took about two years to complete.

I believe God deposits His giftings within us quickly and easily. However, the ways in which He develops and uses those gifts for His glory may be a lengthy and sometimes difficult process.

Oh I know you may get weary
  And the times they may get rough
You may not have all you want
  But you'll always have enough
And when your darkest hour comes
  Just remember what I said
I've never seen the righteous forsaken
  Or their seed begging for bread.

Many of the old writers, the saints from long ago, often referenced a common theme known as "the dark night of the soul." They wrote and spoke of a season or seasons of their lives when it seemed as though God had removed all sense of His presence.

There is little if any tolerance for the mere consideration of such an idea in the midst of our present day "feel good" religious exercises.

Yet the song says, "And when your darkest hour comes." It doesn't say if, it says when. Maybe I should rewrite that line, or perhaps better yet we should see if God's Word supports the assertion.

The oldest manuscript in the Bible tells us of the most righteous man on the planet who enters "the dark night of the soul" by God's own will. In a matter of days Job loses everything – his possessions, his servants, his children and finally his very health. Then his wife shows up and tells him to *"curse God and die."* It's hard to imagine that any of these circumstances would have been perceived by Job as a bright and shining hour. In fact in the midst of it he *"tore his robe and shaved his head"* (an expression of extreme sorrow and shame).

The "darkest hour" drives him to fall to the ground and worship *(Job 1:20).* In his loss and sorrow, Job cursed the day of his birth: *"Let the day perish on which I was to be born, And the night which said, 'A boy is conceived.' May that day be darkness; Let not God above care for it, Nor light shine on it. Let darkness and black gloom claim it; Let a cloud settle on it; Let the blackness of the day terrify it" (Job 3:3-5).*

Yet in his faith, a faith being perfected by the very circumstances assaulting him, he proclaims: *"I know that my Redeemer lives" (Job 19:25).*

He also proclaims, *"Though He slay me, I will hope in Him."* (Some translations say, *"Yet will I trust him") (Job 13:15).*

Another song writer wrote, "The darkest hour means dawn is just in sight."

Moses was cast out of the palace of privilege for a place of poverty as a shepherd in the "south forty" on the back side of nowhere for forty years! It must have been a dark time, but God knew a new day was dawning for His chosen people and their exodus from Egypt would require a well-trained shepherd.

Joseph must have oft contemplated the darkness of his surroundings and circumstances. Literal darkness in the 13 year confinement of a prison. And is there anything more emotionally frustrating than to be wrongly accused?

But in what must have surely been the "dark night of his soul," God is preparing him to save a nation, his family, and the very lineage of the Messiah. From the dark night comes the Light of the World!

I feel somewhat like the writer of Hebrews: *"And what more shall I say? For time will fail me if I tell of Gideon, Barak, Samson, Jepthah, of David and Samuel and the prophets..." (Hebrews 11:32).*

We could recount the stories of the martyrs, the tortures, the imprisonments. We could (and should) consider the present plight of the suffering church in the world. This very day brothers and sisters in Christ, true saints, have been persecuted, suffered and perhaps died for their faith. Yet they wait and trust in God.

Oh I know it seems so hopeless
  And you don't know what to pray
You've done all you know to do
  And it seems there's just no way
And when you feel you're at the end
  Just remember what I said
I've never seen the righteous forsaken
  Or their seed begging for bread.

Most who will read the words of this writing will not be ones who will suffer to the extent of the aforementioned.

Yet suffer, we will, in various ways at various times. I was recently given a book entitled, "Why It Cannot Be God's Will to Suffer." I almost laughed at the absurdity of such a proclamation and then was saddened (and somewhat angered) at the level of scriptural illiteracy and purposed perverting of the Word to come to such a conclusion.

Jesus said, *"Each day will have enough trouble of its own" (Matthew 6:34).* Jesus said, *"In this world you will have trouble (tribulation)" (John 16:33).* Jesus "*learned obedience from the things which He suffered" (Hebrews 5:8).* David wrote, *"Many are the afflictions of the righteous" (Psalm 34:19).*

Yes there is deliverance from the afflictions. Yes we are to take courage for Jesus has overcome the world, but Scripture assures us that in a fallen world and living in corruptible bodies we will face suffering at some time to some degree. *"And after you have suffered for a little while, the God of all grace, who called you to His eternal glory in Christ, will Himself perfect, confirm, strengthen and establish you" (1 Peter 5:10).*

It is all part of the loving disciplinary instruction of a merciful God towards His beloved children.

"For whom the lord loves He disciplines, And He scourges every son whom He receives" (Hebrews 12:6). "All discipline for the moment seems not to be joyful, but sorrowful; yet to those who have been trained by it, afterwards it yields the peaceful fruit of righteousness" (Hebrews 12:11).

So just hold on a little longer
  The answer's soon to come
The endless waiting's almost over
  The victory's almost won
And when again you feel His joy
  You'll remember what I said
I've never seen the righteous forsaken
  Or their seed begging for bread.

There's an old saying that goes, "The hardest part of faith is the last five minutes!" Scripture encourages us to persevere, endure, or as we say, "hang in there!"

David the Psalmist, a shepherd boy, a king, an adulterer and a murderer; a "shedder of blood," but a "man after God's own heart," writes to us from a perspective of many years and many experiences. He has won many victories and has suffered many losses, but he encourages us today by testifying: *"I have been young, and now I am old: Yet I have not seen the righteous forsaken, Or their descendants begging bread" (Psalm 37:25).*

I've never seen God's people
With a need that He could not meet
I know that He cares for His own
And His promises He'll keep.

"Fear not for I am with you, be not dismayed for I am your God, I will strengthen you, I will help you, I will uphold you, with my victorious right hand" (Isaiah 41:10).

I HAVE HOPE

Where do the broken hearted go
  To find a comfort for their pain
So many hurting need to know
  The hope there is in Jesus name.

In July of 1987 my wife, Linda, and I made our first trip down to M D Anderson Cancer Center in Houston, Texas. We would make many more trips in the months and years that would follow, but none would stick in my memory as clearly as that initial visit.

Linda had just been diagnosed with breast cancer and our world was suddenly "turned upside down," as the saying goes. Her biopsy had occurred earlier in the month at a hospital in Tyler, Texas, very near where we live.

When the doctor who performed the biopsy talked with us about his findings, words like lumpectomy, mastectomy, radiation, and chemotherapy became terms nearly as foreign to us as some language from a far away country.

After the initial shock of this jarring experience and these new terms, we were able to catch our breath, so to speak, settle into the sufficient grace that God gives in such moments and find a realm of peace that really does pass our understanding.

From there we were able to begin to assess the landscape of our future journey. After much research and input from others, including some doctors, we felt M D Anderson Cancer Center was to be our next step.

A date was set, a doctor was recommended and assigned and off we went, truly into the realm of the unknown. On the four hour trip from our house to Houston there was plenty of time to talk, pray, wonder and fret, though I know scripture says, *"fret not thyself."*

We played a cassette tape given to us by a friend and fellow singer/songwriter named Terry Clark. One of the songs on that tape would be played many times during our many trips to and from Houston. Titled, "I Am Yours," the words from that song would bathe our hearts and minds with hope.

As Terry sang, "I am Yours, I am Yours, You hold all my life in Your hand," we knew that He did; even this most difficult portion of our life.

I feel I must pause here to tell you that never has a song so specifically impacted my life and ministered to me so profoundly at a desperate time than Terry Clark's "I Am Yours."

We had no idea what awaited us and as is often the tendency of human nature, I'm sure we contemplated some worst case scenarios.

But in the midst of our journey, in the midst of our anxious waiting, we had hope. Our hope was not based on mere wishful thinking, but on the authority and integrity of God's Word.

"My soul waits in silence for God only; From Him is my salvation. He only is my rock and my salvation, My stronghold; I shall not be greatly shaken" (Psalm 62:1-2).

One of my clearest remembrances of those initial hours and days at M D Anderson was the sight of so many of all ages, from all around the world, in every varied degree of condition due to cancer's assault on their bodies.

The most heart wrenching sights were those of little children weak and sickened by both the cancer and the chemotherapy treatments they were enduring in hopes of defeating the disease. Sometimes we would see a child walk by, hooked up to an IV administering their chemo. The child would often use the mobile IV hanger as a support from which to gain aid and balance on their brief walks. A mom and dad would usually be walking beside their child, holding their hand and trying to be strong.

These scenes would cause us to make the same transition in our thoughts as the Psalmist David did when he was being sorely tried and tested.

In Psalm 62 David starts out by testifying about the condition of his soul: *"My soul waits in silence for God only…."* Then as he considers his plight and the turmoil surrounding him, he literally speaks to his own soul.

"My soul, wait in silence for God only, For my hope is from Him. He only is my rock and my salvation, My stronghold; I shall not be shaken" (Psalm 62:5-6).

See the difference? It's rather like the child who might proclaim, "I'm not afraid of anything!" But when they're home alone and the lights suddenly go out, they crouch in a corner and repeat over and over, "I will not be afraid, I will not be afraid!"

The two proclamations are very similar, but the surrounding circumstances have created an entirely new perspective.

When Linda and I would see the scenes of those, especially the little children and their families dealing with cancer, we would often say, "What do people do without Jesus? What do people do without hope in Him?"

We would comfort one another in the fact that though once we were apart from Him, through salvation we had gained Christ and received hope.

But there was also a sense in which we had to strengthen and affirm ourselves in the fact of His hope which now resided within us because of His love.

I tried to make it on my own
  But I kept drifting far away
But now I finally have a home
  In Jesus love I'll always stay.

That's what true hope in Christ is. It's a home, an abode, a secure location if you will.

In Paul's first letter to the church in Corinth, he writes, *"But now abide faith, hope, love, these three; but the greatest of these is love" (1 Corinthians 13:13).*

This chapter, often referred to as the "love chapter," emphasizes love. It gives love a first place priority. However, it in no way diminishes the importance of faith or hope. There is no devaluation of these two foundational components.

We know from scripture, *"And without faith it is impossible to please God..." (Hebrews 11:6),* the writer of Hebrews encourages us as "heirs of the promise" when he writes, *"This hope we have as an anchor of the soul, a hope both sure and steadfast and one which enters within the veil..." (Hebrews 6:19).*

This verse speaks of a hope that is secure, unassailable and both enters and abides within the holiest place.

I have joy in the time of sorrow
  I have peace in the raging storm
I have faith that Jesus holds tomorrow
  I have hope, I'm resting in His arms.

These verses testify to the fact that in all of life's sorrows, storms and concerns about the future, Faith abides! Hope abides! Love abides!

Love is the vehicle which will transport us to our final destination. Faith assures us that even though our journey may be over rough and rocky roads, we will arrive safely. Hope gives us the confidence to rest securely in the comfort of His arms throughout the journey.

I'll carry on till Jesus comes
  Though trials and snares may come my way
And by His strength the race I'll run
  And by His grace these words I'll say.

I have joy in the time of sorrow
  I have peace in the raging storm
I have faith that Jesus holds tomorrow
  I have hope, I'm resting in His arms.

I've often said, "In Christ there are no hopeless situations, but apart from Christ, there is no hope."

Do you have a hope fixed and firm in Christ?

Can you say with the psalmist David, *"My hope is in Thee" (Psalm 39:7)?*

If your hope is in Christ alone, then I can say with all confidence that no matter what you're going through just now, there are no hopeless situations!

Paul writes, *"And hope does not disappoint, because the love of God has been poured out within our hearts through the Holy Spirit who was given to us…" (Romans 5:5).*

Perhaps you know someone who is without hope. Let God's Word instruct us: *"Now we who are strong ought to bear the weaknesses of those without strength and not just please ourselves. Let each of us please his neighbor for his good, to his edification. For even Christ did not please Himself; but as it is written, 'THE REPROACHES OF THOSE WHO REPROACHED THEE FELL UPON ME.' For whatever was written in earlier times was written for our instruction, that through perseverance and the encouragement of the Scriptures we might have hope" (Romans 15:1-4).*

"Hope thou in God…" "Oh remember this: There is never a time when we may not hope in God. Whatever our necessities, however great our difficulties, and though to all appearance help is impos-

sible, yet our business is to hope in God, and it will be found that it is not in vain. In the Lord's own time help will come." (George Mueller)

"Why are you in despair, O my soul? And why have you become disturbed within me? Hope in God, for I shall yet praise Him, The help of my countenance, and my God" (Psalm 42:11).

MOUNT UP WITH WINGS

So many things in life to tie us down
So many ways to keep us on the ground.

I wrote the song, "Mount Up With Wings," in 1988. As I was recalling what circumstances surrounded the inspiration for this song, I couldn't help but rejoice in my now distant perspective from things that once seemed as though they would "tie me down."

On the fourth of July in 1987, Dallas Holm and Praise made a final concert appearance at a festival in Texas. For eleven years we had toured across the country appearing at one time or another in almost every major theater and arena across this land.

Like the old Johnny Cash song, "I've Been Everywhere Man," we too had been just about everywhere it seemed. From maximum security prisons to Madison Square Garden, we had sung and ministered to literally hundreds of thousands of people. It seemed, however, as though "The Times, They Were a Changin", to paraphrase a Bob Dylan song title.

Without going into any details or explanation of how or why things were changing, I just knew they were. It seemed as though God had called and used us in a unique and specific way for a particular season, but I felt very strongly that season was ending.

One need only to open up the Scriptures to find similar accounts of "seasonal" changes in the lives of His people. I am particularly drawn to the story of Elijah, one of God's greatest prophets. I would not want to seem presumptuous in comparing myself to Elijah, and yet I believe such comparisons are not only to be considered, but they are purposed.

I always encourage Christians to study Scripture, especially for two specific reasons. You'll find God and you'll find yourself! You'll find God just as He intended to be revealed and understood through the detailed presentation of writers inspired over the centuries by His Holy Spirit.

You'll also find yourself in the lives of those you read about. Through the accounts and biographies of both the saints of God as well as His enemies, you'll see the common thread throughout history of the plight of mankind.

As Solomon writes so graphically while contemplating the universal realm of vanity, *"That which has been is that which will be, and that which has been done is that which will be done. So, there is nothing new under the sun" (Ecclesiastes 1:9).*

Hence, I identify with this Elijah who seems to just burst on the scene with a sure word from God. He is placed by God before an audience he probably never would have thought possible.

He ministers faithfully the word of the Lord for his audience of one, King Ahab. No sooner has he fulfilled his duty to the King Eternal than he is told by the Lord to *"Go away from here and turn eastward, and hide yourself by the brook Cherith..." (1 Kings 17:3).*

It must have seemed a rather sudden change of plans to go directly from a king to a creek. Interesting to note that as the story continues, we find Elijah's very sustenance being removed. *"And it happened after a while, that the brook dried up, because there was no rain in the land" (l Kings 17:7).*

Well of course, this really should come as no surprise to Elijah, for the very thing he had prophesied to King Ahab was that there would be no rain or dew.

I remember early in my ministry feeling as though God had called me and positioned me to minister to hurting people. I've written many songs in various styles on many topics, but always the return to lyrics designed to bring hope, healing and comfort to God's children.

Once I saw a movie entitled, "The Way We Were," starring Robert Redford and Barbara Streisand. I'm quite sure I would have little in common philosophically, politically or theologically with these Hollywood icons. I did, however, identify with a line early on in the film with amazing familiarity.

In the movie's beginning, Robert Redford is portraying a college student who has submitted a paper for one of his classes. The opening line read: "Things always came too easily for me." When I heard that line, I almost audibly responded in the theater, "I know, me too!"

I had felt this at times as I heard of others who had suffered in this life; Saints who had paid a great price for their faith as the early martyrs, or sometimes friends and family who were struggling with life's assorted difficulties.

I had an intellectual sense of their sorrows and pain, but did not identify much deeper than that.

It's not that I didn't want to, it's that I couldn't, for lack of personal experience. Like Elijah, the very thing I had proclaimed to that special audience in privileged encounters, I would now experience in a personal way.

God seemed to be impressing upon me, "Go away from here... and hide yourself...."

Exactly one week after Dallas Holm and Praise gave their last concert, my wife, Linda, was diagnosed with breast cancer.

Always another worry round the bend.
Sometimes it makes you wonder, when will it ever end?

Never again would I feel, "things always came too easily for me." This was not easy and our lives would change forever. But so too would my understanding and empathy for hurting people. It wasn't just the physical challenges of this time. It seemed all of our life and future was being tested. As concert crowds diminished, record sales trended downward and radio play shifted more to the new young whoever and whatever, it seemed the "brook" was drying up and our very sustenance might be challenged.

By God's grace, others had been lifted up and encouraged through our ministry in music, but now I needed a "lift."

Is there a way to rise above it all
And if there is should I expect to fall?

I desperately wanted to somehow rise above all the things that seemed to have suddenly weighted me down. It wasn't so much that I wanted to fly away from it all, for I believed God was working in all of these circumstances. I needed to be lifted up to gain from His lofty height, a new perspective.

I recently watched a YouTube video of an eagle soaring over some high snow-capped mountains. I certainly have seen videos of eagles flying in the mountains before. In fact I've seen many eagles in my lifetime while out in nature.

However, this one was quite different in that a Go Pro camera had been attached to the eagle so that what you saw was from the eagle's perspective. As he soared over the jagged, inhospitable terrain, I was struck with two things in particular.

First, you could see everything; every rock and crevasse, every deep valley and every distant peak. Secondly, it was so effortless. The eagle seldom flapped his wings. The very canyons that could spell disaster for some wayward traveler were creating the up drafts and thermals that allowed the eagle to soar.

I don't think the eagle had any expectations or concerns of falling, nor should we.

God knew in the very beginning that one of the benefits of the rough, steep and treacherous places He created would be to give flight to the eagle.

Where is there one who'll help me touch the sky
  One who is so much higher
I want to learn to fly.

Mount up with wings, fly like an eagle
  Mount up with wings, soar across the sky
Let your heart sing, fly away from evil
  Come spread your wings, fly eagle fly.

The words to that chorus inspire us to fly, to sing and to soar. And all these things we shall do at times, perhaps in this life and for sure in Heaven forever.

We're assured, however, from scripture, history and experience that effortless flight will not always be our lot in this life.

Storms come, our faith is tested and patience is demanded, but isn't this a good thing? Let's let scripture answer: *"Do you not know? Have you not heard? The Everlasting God, the Lord, the Creator of the ends of the earth does not become weary or tired. His understanding is inscrutable. He gives strength to the weary, and to him who lacks might He increases power. Though youths grow weary and tired, and vigorous young men stumble badly, yet those who wait upon the Lord will gain new strength; they will mount up with wings like eagles, they will run and not get tired, they will walk and not become weary" (Isaiah 40:28-31).*

Sometimes the storms of life will blow you down
Force you to wait in patience on the ground
But waiting before the Lord will make you strong
You're going to fly again after the storm is gone.

"A storm is only as the outskirts of His robe, the symptom of His advent, the environment of His Presence." (F.B. Meyer)

"Bless the Lord, O my soul; And all that is within me, bless His holy name. Bless the Lord, O my soul, and forget none of His benefits; Who pardons all your iniquities; Who heals all your diseases; Who redeems your life from the pit; Who crowns you with loving kindness and compassion; Who satisfies your years with good things, so that your youth is renewed like the eagle" (Psalm 103:1-5).

THIS TOO SHALL PASS

I think the first time I ever heard the phrase, "This too shall pass," it was spoken by my Mother. It was a statement that would come up from time to time in our home to bring hope and encouragement during trying times.

I believe everyone endures trying times and various forms of adversity during the course of their lives. However, it seemed to me, at least when I was younger, that some folks had resources or connections to assist in their difficulties in ways that seemed to belie the very fact that the difficulties even existed.

We didn't have a lot of the kinds of resources that others seemed to possess to buy their way out of, or at least around life's pressing obstacles. Actually I've come to realize that life's trials cannot be "bought off."

Distractions can be purchased in a myriad of ways, but the problems are patient and will generally out wait the distractions until they have disappeared.

Then once again, the "giants" will be faced - those seemingly insurmountable obstacles that life has placed before us.

I don't think as a kid I thought we had the kind of connections that others around us seemed to enjoy. I'm not even sure what I thought "connections" were or how they might be of benefit. I just know that through the eyes of adolescent perception, we seemed to represent the lower range of a small town caste system.

Our neighbors on either side of us had homes with brick, stone, bay windows and normal roof lines. I reference normal roof lines because we had a flat-roof house, the only one in our entire town as I recall. My Mom had seen a flat-roof house once and thought that was a "neat idea." And so when my Dad built our house in the early fifties, he built Mom's "neat idea" house.

In the cold snowy Minnesota winters, Dad often had to go up on the roof and shovel the snow off onto the ground below. Sometimes I wondered how much he liked Mom's neat idea, but I never witnessed a complaint.

Life was simple and I'm sure often hard as my parents sought to raise two boys on the meager salary of a milkman.

If there was financial hardship, pain or sickness, we got through it usually with the encouragement of a simple statement: "This too shall pass!"

For many years I thought that oft-heard saying was a Scripture. I was quite surprised one day to learn it was not. I had heard other quotes through the years, wrongly attributed to Scripture, such as, "God helps those who help themselves" and "God works in mysterious ways." But this sounded really right, and in fact I believe in essence it is, when viewed in the light of other Scriptures.

It is not now, nor would it ever be my intention to elevate any saying or quotation to the level of Scriptural significance.

Yet I believe it may be interesting, if not beneficial, to see whether or not this statement has a basis or a kinship with Scripture's promises.

In the broadest sense, we know that all things are passing away. *"And the world is passing away, and also its lusts; but the one who does the will of God abides forever" (1 John 2:17). "Heaven and earth shall pass away, but my words shall not pass away" (Matthew 24:35).*

Hence, we know everything of a temporal nature, even Heaven and earth, is passing away. But this does not satisfy our desire to know if the difficulty of our present circumstance is assured to desist.

Scripture says, *"Many are the afflictions of the righteous; but the Lord delivers him out of them all" (Psalm 34:19).*

If you and I were to hang around together for any amount of time, you would probably hear me quote that verse. I believe it gives us the clearest and most specific hope to believe that in any and every difficult situation or season there is deliverance.

As they say in the TV commercials, "But wait there's more!" Let's back up a little in that Psalm and gain further encouragement. *"I sought the Lord and He answered me, and delivered me from all my fears" (Psalm 34:4).*

"This poor man cried and the Lord heard him, and saved him out of all his troubles. The angel of the Lord encamps around those who fear Him, and recues them" (Psalm 34:6-7).

"The righteous cry and the Lord hears, and delivers them out of all their troubles. The Lord is near to the broken hearted, and saves those who are crushed in spirit" (Psalm 34:17-18).

I rest my case! No, actually Scripture rests its case on the promises that though we may be afflicted greatly and often, deliverance is assured always and completely.

How and when deliverance comes is not our business, but according to God's Word, which *"shall not pass away,"* deliverance will come.

I guess "this too shall pass" was my Mom's way of consolidating the substance of a vast array of Scriptural promise into a simple phrase of encouragement.

In the late sixties on into the seventies my Mom endured a season of severe depression. She was hospitalized for a period of time, sometimes enduring shock treatments, various protocols and therapies. It was a difficult time for all of us, especially Dad, to wait in patience, pray in faith, and endure the night of depression's darkness, always hoping that joy would come in the morning…at least some morning.

Let me say here that the Christian community has often not handled the realm of depression with wisdom, grace and sensitivity. Sometimes, perhaps with good intentions, the recommendation of the redeemed was to cast out the demon of depression, or just speak against the disease with a sense of denial that would make any Christian Science practitioner proud.

Maybe there was some secret sin from the past that needed to be hunted down, exposed and burned at the stake in classic "witchhunt" fashion.

Don't get me wrong, demons are real and they can oppress and depress. We have a right to stand and fight in faith and on Scripture's authority against all the fiery darts of the enemy.

And sin surely has consequences that can affect us not only spiritually, but emotionally and physically as well.

I fear, however, that too often we have treated those suffering depression as though they were lepers and outcasts, needing to go about crying, "unclean – unclean!"

Charles Haddon Spurgeon, one of God's great ministers and one of the Church's great heroes, suffered with depression throughout much of his life and ministry. He wrote: "I often feel very grateful to God that I have undergone fearful depression of spirits. I know the borders of despair, and the horrible brink of that gulf of darkness into which my feet have almost gone; but hundreds of times I have been able to give a helpful grip to brethren and sisters who have come into that same condition, which grip I could never have given if I had not known their deep despondency. So I believe that the darkest and most dreadful experience of a child of God will help him to be a fisher of men if he will but follow Christ."

My Mom's depression subsided and she returned once again to her energetic, "life-of-the-party" self.

Her affliction was great, the dark valley of depression was deep, but God's deliverance was absolute, as He said it would be.

Perhaps you are even now journeying through the dark valley of depression. Joy seems just beyond your grasp and an emotional numbness has settled in causing you to doubt the coming day of your deliverance. You pray and search Scripture, but the gray days continue.

Friends and loved ones give advice, share particular Scriptural remedies and with all loving concern suggest what you should do, where you should go and why you should try harder.

But "sorrows like sea billows roll." Spurgeon once said: "I could weep by the hour like a child, and yet I knew not what I wept for."May I, as my Mom did many years ago even through her season of depression, consolidate the overwhelming evidence of the volume of Scripture in a simple encouraging statement: Whether here on earth or upon crossing the threshold of Heaven's gate, the assurance of every true believer remains –

This Too Shall Pass

There's a heaviness inside your heart
A weight you can't describe
A feeling that you just can't hide
There's a weariness within your mind
The thoughts don't come to clear
You feel as though I'm not so near to you.

But remember I said I'd never leave
Trust in My Word and believe I am here
Forever, I'll never let you go
This is all you really need to know

I've heard every prayer, I've seen every tear
When I seemed so distant, I've always been near
And I know the future and I know the past
So believe Me when I say, believe Me when I say
This too, this too shall pass.

I know sometimes it's hard for you
To put your trust in Me
To place your faith in what you cannot see
I know sometimes you feel that I'm
A million miles away
But listen to your heart and hear Me say

I've heard every prayer, I've seen every tear
When I seemed so distant, I've always been near

And I know the future and I know the past
  So believe Me when I say, believe Me when I say
This too, this too shall pass.

"O love the Lord, all you His godly ones! The Lord preserves the faithful....Be strong, and let your heart take courage, all you who hope in the Lord" (Psalm 31:23-24).

WORTH THE WAITING

It will be worth the waiting
  All the anticipating
When we see Jesus When we see Jesus
  It will be worth the miles
All of our many trials
  When we see Jesus When we see Jesus.

We're really not good at waiting, for the most part. I think of myself as a patient man because I can sit out in the woods for hours waiting for a deer, elk or some other animal to come by. I can fish from sun-up to sun-down, sometimes with little success and still regard it as a great day.

I have noticed, however, that recently as I wait for that little circular timer on my I-phone or I-pad to stop circling and let me access my emails, weather, or maps, my patience is tested.

We live out in the woods and our internet is pretty slow, so my patience gets a daily workout. Of course, whatever bit of information I'm waiting for usually comes up in less time than it took to dial a phone number on a rotary dial phone not all that many years ago.

Still, every second matters, or so it seems, as the world around us and all its technology is constantly accelerating and leading us to believe we can get more done in less time.

I'm not sure though. I feel like I used to have more time in a day to accomplish more. Now sometimes I feel like I get up, complete two or three tasks and the sun is going down.

My clock indicates there are still twenty four hours in a day, but the hours definitely seem to go by faster.

The days, weeks, and months seem to be picking up speed and the years fly by like some kind of cosmic time-lapse photography.

Some of you may not relate to this assessment, but I know some of you will. I thought maybe it was just because I'm getting older, but even my grandkids think the years go by pretty fast. Of course for them that's a good thing because Christmas gets here sooner.

I'm sure nothing has changed within the actual realm of time measurement, but I believe the closer we get to the end of time and Christ's return, our perspective changes greatly.

Sometimes I get so tired
  That I just want to go away
Wish He would come and take me home today
  Being with Him would be better
But for you I will choose to stay
  A little bit longer so you might know the way.

Sound familiar? Paul wrestled with this same dilemma almost two thousand years ago. *"But I am hard-pressed from both directions, having the desire to depart and be with Christ, for that is very much better; yet to remain on in the flesh is more necessary for your sake" (Philippians 1:23-24).*

The apostle Paul wrote these words believing that his time on earth may soon be over, as he was awaiting trial in a Roman prison. Contemplating the possibility of seeing his Saviour soon was surely a joyous anticipation. And yet he was torn because of those he loved on earth and for whom he had a great desire to nurture in their growth in grace.

Shouldn't this be representative of our juxtaposition as well? We live at the threshold of His coming, inciting great joy at the thought of our eternal union with Him in Heaven and all that will mean.

Yet because of the urgent sensing of that which will soon be, we desire more time to accomplish more for Him now, especially in the lives of those we love and those who by His love will be brought across our path.

We live with a very real understanding of the old saying, "So little time, so much to do." Then there are also times in our lives when we wish we could speed up the clock!

I remember as a boy taking trombone lessons, how I wished time would move a little faster. Because I had a private lesson every week, every month for many years, I had to do a lot of practicing. Daily! Scales, intervals, double tonguing, triple tonguing (bet you're wondering what that is if you don't play a brass instrument) in different keys day after day. I was supposed to practice one hour a day and I did, at least for awhile.

My parents would set the manual twist timer on the stove in the kitchen. I would then descend downstairs into the dungeon of doom to practice my trombone in the basement.

One day as I was particularly bored in my dismal discipline, I noticed I could hear where my parents were upstairs by the sound of their footsteps and the creaking hardwood floor beneath their feet. They were in the bedroom at the other end of the house from the kitchen! I guess I've always been creative, even before I was a Christian. What seemed at the time to be a brilliant idea, formed in my mind.

Slowly, carefully, and silently like a cat I crept up the stairs of my torture cell, opened the door into the kitchen ever so slowly and tiptoed like some cat burglar across the linoleum floor to the stove.

As a safecracker would gently caress the combination dial on a safe, I carefully gripped the timer dial and moved it counter-clockwise five minutes. Then as in one of those movies where the safecracker suddenly hears police sirens outside the bank and hastily makes his escape, I too made a hasty escape back down to the basement.

My heart was pounding, my throat was dry and I sat in silence for what seemed like an eternity, expecting to hear footsteps running from Mom and Dad's bedroom to the kitchen to the downstairs where they would both, with utter disbelief, demand to know what in the world I had just done! But it never happened. And I mean never happened, even when I began to sneak upstairs and dial ten to fifteen minutes off the timer.

I guess at the time I thought I was pretty smart. Sin is always greatly deceitful. Years later I confessed my sin to my parents and all was well.

But really, what was the outcome of my time manipulation? I practiced less, so I was a little less proficient in my trombone ability. When I thought I was winning I was losing. And so it is always when we step in and try to manipulate God's laws, plans and purposes.

I read this recently: "Cease meddling with God's plans and will. You touch anything of His and you mar the work. You may move the hands of the clock to suit you, but you do not change the time; so you may hurry the unfolding of God's will, but you harm and do not help the work." (Stephen Merritt)

So here we are at a most critical juncture of time and history. We well may be those who live in the final ticks of the clock and this may tempt us to set the timer forward a little to speed things up, or so it would seem.

I believe it is possible to miss present potential for peering prematurely into the promised land.

There's an old saying that goes, "You can be so Heavenly minded that you're of no earthly good." I've never really liked that statement because I don't think you can be too Heavenly minded.

The Bible says, *"Set your mind on the things above, not on the things that are on earth" (Colossians 3:2).*

Scripture also says, *"Do not lay up for yourselves treasures upon earth, where moth and rust destroy, and where thieves break in and steal. But lay up for yourselves treasures in Heaven…" (Matthew 6:19-20).*

I believe it's possible to be so earthly minded you're of no Heavenly good! But this is not what I'm talking about when I reference peering prematurely into the promised land.

Let's look at the apostle Paul again for our example. Consider Paul's ministry, its hardships and its challenges: *"Five times I received from the Jews thirty-nine lashes. Three times I was beaten with rods, once I was stoned, three times I was shipwrecked, a night and a day I have spent in the deep. I have been on frequent journeys, in dangers from rivers, dangers from robbers, dangers from my countrymen, dangers from the Gentiles, dangers in the city, dangers in the wilderness, dangers on the sea, dangers among false brethren; I have been in labor and hardship, through many sleepless nights, in hunger and thirst, often without food, in cold and exposure..." (2 Corinthians 11:24-27).*

The list goes on, but you get the picture. So now, towards the end of his life's journey, imprisoned, tired and worn, surely looking forward to his Heavenly home, it would have been so easy to pass over the present potential and begin to prematurely peer into the promised land. He could have sought to move the timer just a little to avoid the discipline of the dungeon. But he didn't!

Instead, he believed that all present concerns and opportunities as well as future eternal peace was worth the waiting so that God could accomplish His purposes through him.

And from his imprisonments we receive epistles (letters) helping to form the very basis of our faith and foundation of our beliefs.

In Ephesians he writes, *"For by grace you have been saved through faith; and that not of yourselves, it is the gift of God; not as a result of works, that no one should boast" (Ephesians 2:8-9).*

In Philippians he teaches us by the Holy Spirit, *"For to me, to live is Christ, and to die is gain" (Philippians 1:21).*

Reflecting on his life and ministry he writes, *"I count all things to be loss in view of the surpassing value of knowing Christ Jesus my Lord, for whom I have suffered the loss of all things, and count them but rubbish in order that I may gain Christ" (Philippians 3:8).*

In Colossians he helps us to see who this Christ is: *"For in Him all the fullness of Deity dwells in bodily form, and in Him you have been made complete, and He is the head over all rule and authority" (Colossians 2:9-10).*

Then in Philemon, Paul, by way of a beautiful analogy, demonstrates the love and forgiveness of Christ. A slave named Onesimus is guilty of a great offense. Paul willingly lays aside his own rights and becomes Onesimus's substitute by assuming his debt.

All these things and more, the early Christians and we today learn, embrace and cherish because Paul was willing to wait on God's time, believing that all that was presently transpiring and that which lay ahead would be worth the waiting.

Standing in His presence there'll be love and perfect peace
Cloudy days will all have passed away
Nothing to alarm us nothing there can harm us
Living in that never-ending day.
It will be worth the waiting
All the anticipating
When we see Jesus When we see Jesus
It will be worth the miles
All of our many trials
When we Jesus When we see Jesus

"For I consider that the sufferings of this present time are not worthy to be compared with the glory that is to be revealed to us" (Romans 8:18).

HEAL ME

Back in the late 70's I had the privilege to go elk hunting up on the Grand Mesa outside of Grand Junction, Colorado. I suppose next to my love for the Lord and my wife and family, there are few if any things I enjoy more than the great outdoors. I love to fish, hunt, backpack and explore as much of God's marvelous creation as I can.

So the chance to go by horseback up into the snowy mountains of Colorado on a great hunting adventure was enough to keep me awake at night, at least when I wasn't dreaming about bull elk.

The trip was all I imagined and more, which I would not have thought possible.

In a veritable snow- covered winter wonderland, we were camped out in a tent at almost 10,000 ft. The beaver pond right next to us provided us with some tasty trout at meal time.

This was the stuff dreams are made of, at least the dreams of those who love the outdoors.

I'll not share the story of the elk hunt itself, for as it turned out that was not the most memorable moment of the adventure.

Though I was successful in that endeavor (harvesting an elk), it was another experience God gave me which ultimately was catalogued and stored higher on the shelves of my memory banks.

One afternoon, about the third day of the hunt, I had hiked, climbed and crawled up to a high vantage point from which I could glass a great distance. Perched on a piece of rock protruding out from a steep cliff, I could see down to a valley below, a hillside across and woods all around.

Suddenly, as a mother would pull the blanket up over her sleeping child, God pulled in a blanket of clouds from the valley behind and below me. In mere moments, everything I had just been observing was gone in an instant!

There I was on that piece of rock just above the bank of clouds. The valley below was gone, the hillside across was completely shrouded and not a tree in sight anywhere!

It really was reminiscent of one of those scenes from a movie where someone has ascended into the clouds of Heaven, alone and wondering.

I was both thrilled and somewhat apprehensive. Thrilled to witness such a sight, which I have never seen before or since, and apprehensive as I considered the prospects of making my way back down to camp with minimal visibility.

Then I saw something far off in the distance. It was a mountain range. Jagged snow-capped peaks thrust their way up through the same bank of clouds I was looking down upon. A reference point! And at this point it was the only other object in my entire world that wasn't cloaked in clouds. I tried to imagine how much taller those mountains were than my vantage point and how far away they must be.

I wondered how long a journey it would take to reach them and how difficult it would be under the canopy of such thick cloud cover. (I learned later the mountains I had seen were almost one hundred miles away.)

In the midst of all my wonderings, just as suddenly as the clouds had rolled in, they rolled right back out. Once again I could see everything around and below me. I could still see the mountain range far off and it struck me that I hadn't noticed it previously. It took the covering of all else to fix my attention on an impressive reference point. Some years later, this experience found its way into a song:

I knew life had its valleys
  Never thought that it would not be so
But even if they'd told me
  I never would've thought they'd be this low
I've stood upon the mountain
  Looked across to higher peaks and more
But the only way to reach them
  Is to journey through the lowly valley floor.

Approximately ten years after the mountain adventure I just described to you, I would embark on another journey. This time the clouds would be over me and the valley would be my vantage point.

In July of 1987 my wife, Linda, was diagnosed with cancer. Multifocal Infiltrating Ductal Carcinoma they called it. Cancer was the only word I really heard from the doctor following the biopsy.

Linda had detected a lump in her breast that was accompanied by occasional discomfort. The doctor tried to assure us before the biopsy that "these things are rarely malignant." However, as he came through the door into the waiting room following the procedure, I sensed in his countenance a more ominous pronouncement was about to be offered. And it was.

In rather stoic, clinical fashion, he explained what he had found and what may lie ahead. I remember thinking that it seemed our lives had just come to a screeching halt and I had no idea what the next step was going to be.

I walked from the waiting room to the room they would bring her to after recovery. I tried to hold my emotions together as I passed people in the hallway. This is what outdoorsmen of the adventuresome kind do.

However, when I arrived at her room, I went into the bathroom, shut the door and sobbed like a baby. What would happen now? Would Linda be all right? Was she going to live or was she going to die?

I had certainly heard of cancer, prayed for people with cancer and had known some who died of cancer; but I really didn't know anything about it at all. But together we would learn.

All the details pertaining to the disruption of our lives at this time are not necessary to discuss here. Linda did have surgery, underwent chemo, lost all her beautiful hair and lived for many months in that state of fatigue and sickness that a chemo protocol often presents.

Our lives seemed to be moving in slow motion as we walked day by day in the valley of the unknown. We said at one point it seemed our lives had been reduced to a series of five minute increments as we waited for test results, calls from nurses, appointment schedules and so on.

One evening in the midst of this difficult and seemingly endless journey, I went out to my studio and wrote a song. When it was completed I asked Linda to come out and give it a listen. I placed a pair of headphones on her beautiful bald head, sat at the piano and as she stood behind me I sang the words to "Heal Me."

She listened to the first verse, which I've already shared with you. Then in the midst of our slow motion journey, I sang for her the second verse:

How long have I been traveling
  Days or years, sometimes I just don't know
And how deep is this valley
  And how many more miles must I go
My body's growing weary
  Seems my strength has all but slipped away
Oh God You've got to help me
  Place Your healing hand on me today.

This wasn't just a song, this was a prayer, a desperate cry from deep within to lead us through and out of this valley of the shadow of death!

Heal me, touch me with Your love
  Heal me, send Your Spirit from above and
Hear me, help me Lord I pray
  Jesus come and make me whole today.

Linda has often testified that in that moment of hearing "Heal Me" for the first time she realized that when you go through these "valley" experiences you take everyone you love right along with you.

The journey now has continued for almost three decades. The cancer has had to be re-addressed along the way with more surgeries, radiation and various treatments.

Linda enjoys great health. Once she wondered if she would live to see our children graduate from school. We've seen both our daughter, Jennifer, and our son, Jeffrey, graduate, marry and have children, our five grandchildren!

Some would say it's been a sad journey. We would disagree, for "*in our weakness, His strength is perfected.*" We heartily agree with Paul: *"My grace is sufficient for you, for power is perfected in weakness. Most gladly, therefore, I will rather boast about my weaknesses, that the power of Christ may dwell in me...for when I am weak, then I am strong" (2 Corinthians 12:9-10).*

I have been on the mountain top and I have been in the valley, both literally and figuratively. Some would say, "Surely life above the clouds is to be desired over life beneath them." I would respond by saying, life is best lived and appreciated wherever God in His infinite love and mercy has sovereignly placed you.

Oswald Chambers said: "Don't complain you're of no use where you are for you are certainly of no use where you're not." (My Utmost for His Highest).

After all, what are the clouds? Nahum says, *"...clouds are the dust beneath His feet" (Nahum 1:3).* Therefore, clouds are the very evidence of His presence.

We know from scripture that He goes before us, He is by our side, He is our rear guard, He undergirds us and He sings over us.

I like to say, "He's got you covered!"

Dear soul, are you in a dark valley just now, overcast by a cloud bank that rolled in suddenly? Do you long to gain a lofty perch above the nebula, perchance to gain some distant point of reference?

Be encouraged, *"The Lord is near to the broken hearted, and saves those who are crushed in spirit" (Psalm 34:18).*

His grace IS sufficient and He IS faithful!

Oh God I know You're faithful
  Leading me each step every day
But sometimes in the valley
  I just forget You've often passed this way
The path is steep and narrow
  Seems this upward climb will never stop
So I'm holding on to You Lord
  And in Your strength I know I'll make the top.

"Even though I walk through the valley of the shadow of death, I fear no evil; for Thou art with me; Thy rod and Thy staff, they comfort me" (Psalm 23:4).

IF ALL I EVER KNEW

Believing in the things you cannot see
  Is hard sometimes but it's the way for me
Cause things I saw began to fall
  And slowly fade away
But things the Lord has shown to me
  Are in my heart to stay.

This song explores in a relatively brief and poetic way the huge realm of faith. There is much talk these days of faith. One need only to surf the Christian TV channels to find a veritable plethora of faith teaching, preaching and marketing of all things related directly or indirectly to faith.

I fear, however, that too often the "faith" that's being dispensed as quickly and easily as peanuts at the ball park, is a far cry from true biblical faith.

Perhaps to best understand biblical faith we should take a look at what is unbiblical faith. I often refer to this as "Genie in the lamp" faith!

Remember the story of Aladdin, who comes across a magic lamp? In some versions of this story Aladdin rubs the lamp, in others he utters magic words while rubbing. Some accounts reference two genies, one greater than the other. But in all accounts, the Genie, however he is summoned, appears and exists to do the bidding of the one who possesses the lamp.

Much of the errant presentation of faith that is so popular these days would seem to suggest that the Bible is as that magic lamp. One need not necessarily open it and investigate its contents, but rather just handle it in a way that glosses over or rubs it externally. The promises of God are treated as magical incantations to not only summon the One who made the promises, but to also remind Him of what He promised (as though He may have forgotten).

There is an arrogance and self centeredness to this kind of faith that is truly breathtaking! The last time I checked, we don't tell God what He needs to do for us; He tells us what we need to do for Him, who we are to be in Him, and how we are to relate to others.

"And he answering said, 'Thou shalt love the Lord thy God with all thy heart, and with all thy soul, and with all thy strength, and with all thy mind; and thy neighbor as thyself'" (Luke 10:27).

Could anyone wish for anything of greater value than eternal life in a perfect state in a perfect place called Heaven? This scripture was given in response to the question put forth to Jesus, *"Teacher, what must I do to inherit eternal life?" (Luke 10:25).*

Jesus responds with what would seem to be a fairly straight forward and concise answer. However, a few words from Jesus speak volumes to us and begin to unlock our understanding into the realm of true faith. In this short verse He shows us our complete dependence on Him, the absolute necessity of total abandonment of ourselves to Him, and the humble commitment to love and serve others with the same regard as we would have for ourselves.

So if all I ever knew is what He told me
 If all I ever saw is what He showed me
I'd be content to realize He knows me
 And all I'd want to do is live for Him.

True faith is not so much about getting things from God in answer to our prayers as it is in just trusting God until the answer comes. And even if the answer doesn't come, at least in the way we thought it should, we will still trust Him by faith.

Here's a specific and reasonable question for each of us. Do we really want to please God? Scripture says, *"And without faith it is impossible to please God…" (Hebrews 11:6).* So what is faith? *"Now faith is the substance of things hoped for, the evidence of things not seen" (Hebrews 11:1).*

Here is good news! Faith is substance and evidence! It is not the mystical, ethereal wisp of a cloud that seems to hover somewhere just beyond our reach. It is tangible, it is real and it may be grasped.

Faith is made of things you cannot see
 But things that in my heart I know must be
To put my faith in things above
 Is all that I can do
In Heaven's hope and Jesus' love
 The things I know are true.

How do we know Heaven's hope and Jesus' love are true? We have not been to Heaven and we have as yet not seen Jesus. We believe these things to be true because God's Word tells us so.

Our faith is built upon the foundation of the substance and evidence of God's Word. *"So faith comes from hearing, and hearing by the word of Christ" (Romans 10:17).* That verse begins with a "so." This indicates that something was written prior to this verse which sets up the statement of conclusion.

It's much like an attorney, who in wrapping up his summary remarks might say, "So in conclusion."

This statement urges us to take into serious consideration all that was previously said.

What was previously written? *"WHOEVER WILL CALL UPON THE NAME OF THE LORD WILL BE SAVED" (Joel 2:32). "How then shall they call upon Him in whom they have not believed? And how shall they believe in Him whom they have not heard? And how shall they hear without a preacher? And how shall they preach unless they are sent? Just as it is written, 'HOW BEAUTIFUL ARE THE FEET OF THOSE WHO BRING GLAD TIDINGS OF GOOD THINGS'" (Romans 10:13-15).*

One of the most important segments of the previous scripture is, *"Just as it is written."* This speaks to substance and evidence! It is written. It is recorded. It can be verified.

Do you know there is more historical, archaeological and manuscriptural evidence for Christianity than all other religions of the world combined? Yet it is not proof that turns the soul from sin, it is faith.

Our lives, our beliefs and our faith rest securely on the authority, integrity and sufficiency of God's Word.

We believe in Jesus because we heard the gospel and believed it to be true. Of course we would not have heard and believed if we had not been drawn. *"No one can come to Me, unless the Father who sent Me draws him..." (John 6:44).*

So God sends those who will proclaim the message of the gospel and He draws those who will hear and respond. And yet it is only by His grace that we are able to respond and receive. *"For by grace you have been saved through faith; and that not of yourselves, it is the gift of God; not as a result of works, that no one should boast" (Ephesians 2:8-9).*

In this we realize the very core issue of our salvation rests on faith. And so every other issue of our lives, our beliefs and our eternal hope rests solely on faith. We believe, by faith, that God is Who His Word says He is and that all His Word proclaims is true.

Therefore, we may be free from sin, that thing which would keep us eternally separated from God. *"If you abide in My word, then you are truly disciples of Mine; and you shall know the truth, and the truth shall make you free" (John 8:31-32). "If therefore the Son shall make you free, you shall be free indeed" (John 8:36).*

Is it any wonder that the thing Satan most desires to attack is our faith? If our faith rests on the truth of God's Word to make us free, then it follows that any destruction of our faith will lead to bondage and fear.

Hence, the false teachers who seem to abound these days, promoting their "Genie in the lamp" faith teaching, are to be pitied, exposed and denounced.

If you think I'm being hard on them, listen to the apostle Peter as he denounces false teachers: *"But these, (false teachers) like unreasoning animals born as creatures of instinct to be captured and killed, reviling where they have no knowledge, will in the destruction of those creatures also be destroyed, suffering wrong as the wages of doing wrong. They count it a pleasure to revel in the daytime. They are stains and blemishes, reveling in their deceptions, as they carouse with you, having eyes full of adultery, and that never cease from sin, enticing unstable souls, having a heart trained in greed, accursed children; forsaking the right way they have gone astray… For speaking out arrogant words of vanity they entice by fleshly desires, by sensuality, those who barely escape from the ones who live in error, promising them freedom while they themselves are slaves of corruption…" (II Peter 2:12-19).*

Perhaps your faith is being tested just now. And to add insult to injury, you struggle because someone showed you how to "rub the magic lamp" to get your wishes. But as yet your wishes and requests have not been realized.

Maybe you are under the impression that if your faith is being tested, there must be something wrong, perhaps because of sin in your life.

Spurgeon said: "A faith not tested is no faith at all!"

Oswald Chambers said: "Faith by its very nature must be tested."

James, by the inspiration of the Holy Spirit writes: *"Consider it all joy, my brethren, when you encounter various trials, knowing that the testing of your faith produces endurance. And let endurance have its perfect result, that you may be perfect and complete, lacking in nothing" (James 1:2-4).*

False teachers tell us there should be no testing of our faith nor struggle in our lives. Instant gratification should be our expectation.

God tells us there <u>will</u> be struggle and trial, and this should be considered with joy. Remember, *"For the joy of the Lord is your strength" (Nehemiah 8:10).*

He ensures our faith will be tested, but encourages us to embrace the endurance that this testing will produce, for through it we will be perfected and completed.

Finally, we will have no lack! This has little to do with material things and everything to do with "*the riches in Christ Jesus,*" which silver and gold could never purchase.

This is real faith, biblical faith, faith that trusts Him, in and through every situation. True faith desires to know only that which He speaks, to see only that which He has demonstrated and to yield to His absolute control.

So if all I ever knew is what He told me
If all I ever saw is what He showed me
If all He wants to do is just control me
Then all I want to do is live for Him.

"By faith we understand that the worlds were prepared by the word of God, so that what is seen was not made out of things which are visible" (Hebrews 11:3).

HE'LL DRY THE TEARS

He'll dry the tears from your eyes
He'll take the pain from your heart
He'll move the clouds from your skies
He'll dry the tears from your eyes.

"And I saw the holy city, new Jerusalem, coming down out of Heaven from God, made ready as a bride adorned for her husband. And I heard a loud voice from the throne saying, 'Behold the tabernacle of God is among men, and He shall dwell among them, and they shall be His people, and God himself shall be among them, and He shall wipe away every tear from their eyes; and there shall no longer be any mourning, or crying, or pain; the first things have passed away'" (Revelation 21:2-4).

Matthew Henry offers beautiful commentary on this passage of scripture: "This new and blessed state will be free from all trouble and sorrow; for all the effects of former trouble shall be done away. They have been often before in tears, by reason of sin, of affliction, of the calamities of the church; but now all tears shall be wiped away; no signs, no remembrance of former sorrows shall remain, any further than to make their present felicity the greater. All the causes of future sorrow shall be forever removed."

This beautiful passage of scripture and commentary gives us a hope of future joy, happiness and eternal unsullied bliss that quite frankly is beyond our comprehension.

We have lived all our lives in a fallen world and in a corruptible body, and sorrow and tears have oft been our frequent companion.

We rejoice in the promise scripture gives us, to know we are surely destined to abide forever in a state of perfect joy and harmony if we have trusted, by faith in Christ and have endured till the end.

But what we would also like to know is whether there is reason to hope that in our current state, with its often tearful moments, we have reason to hope for present relief.

He knows the way that you feel
  He's felt the weight that you bear
He knows it's all very real
  He knows the way that you feel
For He is touched with the feelings of our weaknesses
  He has been there too
In your despair remember all His promises
  He will see you through.

"For we have not an high priest which cannot be touched with the feeling of our infirmities; but was in all points tempted like as we are, yet without sin. Let us therefore come boldly unto the throne of grace, that we may obtain mercy, and find grace to help in time of need" (Hebrews 4:15-16).

This passage of scripture has always given me tremendous hope, comfort and encouragement. It assures me that Jesus, our high priest, has more than just a knowledge of the things we are going through. That would be comforting in and of itself. However, it goes on to say that He is intimately acquainted with all the feelings, emotional challenges and even temptations that can accompany our moments and seasons of infirmity.

This text does not suggest He went through these things in some other way, contrary to our experience, but rather, *"like as we are."*

The temptations that assault us, due to the weakness and infirmity of our flesh, along with all related feelings of emotional angst, persist to confront us at every point, in every way and at any time.

As we consider the fact that He was tempted in "all points," our minds race to consider the ways in which we are tempted. Too numerous to list, right?

But was He tempted to despair?

Let's look to scripture. I believe it can be argued that perhaps the most critical juncture of Christ's life and earthly ministry occurred in the Garden of Gethsemane.

If Jesus doesn't press through in prayer, laying aside His own will and surrendering to the Father's will, there is no cross, no atoning blood, and no resurrection.

In Matthew's account of what transpired in the Garden, he writes Jesus' words: *"My soul is deeply grieved, to the point of death..." (Matthew 26:38).*

Jesus goes on to say, *"My Father, if it is possible, let this cup pass from Me..." (Matthew 26:39).*

I think it's noteworthy that only a few chapters previous to this, Jesus assures His disciples that, *"...with God all things are possible" (Matthew 19:26).*

And this reassuring statement harkens all the way back to Genesis where Moses, in relaying the story of Abraham and Sarah, writes, *"Is anything too difficult for the Lord?" (Genesis 18:14).*

Jesus doesn't just know the word, He is the Living Word! Yet in the extreme difficulty of His circumstance, the Son of God contemplates what may not be possible.

This is a desperate prayer, a cry from the deepest depths of anguish and conflict.

Is it not a great comfort to know that wherever we may tread, He has gone before? In all of life's journey we will never come to a place that He has not first surveyed in length and breadth, in height and depth, and passed through victoriously.

How is this made possible? Ironically it is possible because the One who prayed, *"if it is possible,"* concluded His prayer with the words that should be our pattern for every prayer – *"...yet not as I will, but as Thou wilt" (Matthew 26:39).*

Thus, He invites us to come with boldness to the very throne of grace with an expectation to receive mercy and grace to help in our time of need.

What a hope and comfort we have in Christ!

He'll never leave you alone
He'll always stay by your side
A friend like you've never known
He'll never leave you alone.

It would be enough to know He had gone before, pioneered the trail and conquered all our foes. And this He has done, but He continues to be, *"...a very present help in trouble" (Psalm 46:1).*

He tells us as believers, *"You are my friends, if you do what I command you. No longer do I call you slaves...but I have called you friends" (John 15:14-15).*

"I will never desert you, nor will I ever forsake you" (Hebrews 13:5).

By the declaration of His Word and the presence of His Holy Spirit within us, we as believers can have complete assurance that we are not only sons and daughters of the living God, but friends as well.

Scripture assures us that though we may feel alone and circumstances may seem to suggest we have surely been forsaken, we never need cry, *"My God, why hast Thou forsaken me?"*

Jesus was not forsaken on the cross and we will never be forsaken in this life or the life to come. How do I know? The Bible tells me so, as we used to sing so confidently as little children.

We know in this life there will be suffering, adversity and sorrow. To not know this is to not know God's Word. To not know this is to be either woefully ignorant or in a realm of denial that defies comprehension.

An invitation to boldly approach God's throne, *"to obtain mercy and find grace to help in time of need"* makes it clear, there will be times of need!

And the times of need in our lives will be such that only God's marvelous grace will suffice.

But it will suffice! For He has said, *"My grace is sufficient for you..." (II Corinthians 12:9).*

As parents, we remember times when after tending to the bumps and bruises, cuts and scrapes, and hurt feelings of our little children, we would say, "OK now, let's dry those tears."

If we as loving parents know the value of wiping away tears, doesn't it follow that God knows also? He'll dry the tears from your eyes!

"Blessed are you who weep now, for you shall laugh" (Luke 6:21).

HE KNEW ME THEN

Through the years I've often been asked, "Of all the songs you've written, which one is your favorite?" My response has always been to say that if God somehow impressed upon me to pick one of my songs and that would be the only song of mine I could sing from now on, I would choose, "He Knew Me Then."

I'm sure I've never written a more simple song than this one. Both lyrically and musically it is so uncomplicated that it might barely gain one's attention in its structure and form.

However, in its presentation of the essence of the Gospel, we are reminded that the reality of the love of God, as expressed on Calvary's cross, may be grasped by any and all because of the very simplicity of the message itself.

The Apostle Paul, highly educated and divinely appointed, was more than adequately prepared to plumb the depths of any complex theological debate.

Yet in his letter to the church in Corinth he writes: *"And when I came to you, brethren, I did not come with superiority of speech or of wisdom, proclaiming to you the testimony of God. For I determined to know nothing among you except Jesus Christ, and Him crucified" (1 Corinthians 2:1-2).*

In this, Paul is certainly not stating some choice of willful ignorance or a commitment to discuss nothing other than Christ's crucifixion. We know from all his writings that he, by the inspiration of the Holy Spirit, helps to construct the very framework of our faith in great detail.

Perhaps more than any other writer, he helps us to understand God's eternal and pre-ordained purposes for "the Body of Christ" (the true Church) in regards to redemption, calling, function and eternal destiny.

Paul explains to us the transition from the Law to Grace. He instructs us regarding spiritual gifting and church discipline. He confronts the intellectual and religious elite and at the same time compassionately mentors the young Timothy.

Paul was a man fully engaged in the complexities of living as a Christian on earth while holding a citizenship in Heaven.

His ministry has had a profound impact on Christianity through the ages and the world itself. Yet at the center of all his life and ministry was a simple focus and commitment to the Gospel message as expressed on the cross.

Toward the end of his life and ministry, as he reflects upon his obedience to God's call and the hardships that have accompanied that call, he writes: *"But none of these things move me, neither count I my life dear unto myself, so that I might finish my course with joy, and the ministry, which I have received of the Lord Jesus, to testify the gospel of the grace of God" (Acts 20:24).*

He knew me then, He knows me now
  And He died for me
He loved me then, He loves me now
  Oh how can it be
He saw my face, He knew the place
  That I would be today
He knew me then, He knows me now
  And He loves me.

I remember hearing a quote years ago that went, "If I were the only one who ever sinned, Christ still would have died for me."

Though God knew before the foundation of the world that it would not be only I who sinned but that all would sin, still He desired intimate relationship with you and with me. Thus He initiated a plan to redeem, reconcile and literally rebirth those who would otherwise die in their trespasses and sin.

When I was young I used to think the message of the Gospel was that which pertained only to the Scriptural accounts found in the four "Gospels" of Matthew, Mark, Luke and John.

However, now after many years of walking with God, studying His Word and growing in grace, I realize that all of Scripture pertains to and presents the Gospel message. Every book, every chapter and every verse is carefully and beautifully woven together as a great eternal tapestry to fix our attention on the central issue of the substitutionary atoning work of Calvary's cross.

"Christ and Him crucified!"

At the time of the writing of this chapter, I am presently reading and studying the book of Numbers. Having just completed going through Leviticus in the course of my daily devotional studies, I am wishing I would have signed up for that speed reading course they used to offer on TV.

They promised you would be able to read so much faster while at the same time retaining a far greater amount of what you read.

I guess it might be valuable to know and retain the fact that Eliasaph, the son of Deuel, and his army numbered 45,650.

Likewise, knowing that an omer is a tenth of an ephah could come in handy in the right circumstance, though probably not in East Texas where I live.

Just the other day I was reading the instructions given by God to Moses and Aaron concerning the duties of the sons of Kohath, Gershon and Merari when it came to packing up and moving the tabernacle.

First, Aaron and his sons had to know how to pack up all the dishes, pans, sacrificial bowls, snuffers, oil vessels and all the holy things of the tabernacle. Then some are covered with porpoise skins, some with a blue cloth, and on and on it goes.

Finally the sons of Kohath, Gershon and Merari are instructed how to carry all those things properly, *"...that they may live and not die when they approach the most holy objects..." (Numbers 4:19).*

"But they shall not go in to see the most holy objects even for a moment, lest they die" (Numbers 4:20).

When I read that I thought, I never would have made it. I would have had to peek in or I would put the porpoise skin on the wrong things or carried something improperly, and suddenly... poof, no more Dallas!

So what is this all about? Why did God inspire Moses to record all this detailed information (and so much more) for us to consider thousands of years later?

The short answer is that it took a 1,500 year illustrated sermon by God to show mankind that the Law with all its detailed information, specific demands and carefully itemized instructions could not fully accomplish the ransom necessary to once and for all atone for the sin of man.

The old covenant, slowly and methodically, began to open our dulled minds to the concept of holiness versus the profane.

We began to understand that there was nothing we could do in our own strength, even in proper response to clearly articulated divine law, that could truly satisfy God's justice concerning sin.

The sacrifice of animals taught us that there must be a sacrifice, and blood must be shed for atonement. *"And according to the Law, one may almost say, all things are cleansed with blood, and without shedding of blood there is no forgiveness" (Hebrews 9:22).*

Finally the stage is set for the perfect Lamb of God. *"Behold the Lamb of God who takes away the sin of the world!" (John 1:29).*

There's no way John (the Baptist), others witnessing the scene that day, nor us today, can fully appreciate the enormous impact of that pronouncement.

The writer of Hebrews helps us to understand: *"But when Christ appeared as a high priest of the good things to come, he entered through the greater and more perfect tabernacle, not made with hands, that is to say, not of this creation; and not through the blood of goats and calves, but through His own blood, he entered the holy place once for all, having obtained eternal redemption" (Hebrews 9:11-12).*

Once for all! Eternal redemption! What huge and wonderful truths! And yet some stand idly by and speculate, as did those who lined the streets the day He carried the cross to Golgotha's hill.

Some, that day, had no doubt heard Him teach and perhaps had seen or heard of one of the miracles He had performed.

They had been privy to conversations concerning the coming Messiah and perhaps had even been persuaded that Jesus might be the One.

After Jesus passed by, bleeding profusely from the blows, the crown of thorns and the scourging, many undoubtedly stepped in the street behind and followed after to observe what was to come of this Man.

In following, they stepped in the blood of the very One who would atone for their sins. Within hours, as they each went to their homes after witnessing the brutal spectacle of a crucifixion, they would remove their sandals, and the atoning blood of the Lamb of God would dry on the bottoms of their footwear.

They had no idea what they had witnessed, where they had walked and Whom they had seen.

But we do! And yet, some still stand on the side and speculate.

Some people say that He died one day
    But that was long ago
Well I'm sure that He was a very good man
    But me He did not know.

Scripture says otherwise. He does know us and knows us well.

"For Thou didst form my inward parts; Thou didst weave me in my mother's womb...My frame was not hidden from Thee, when I was made in secret....Thine eyes have seen my unformed substance; and in Thy book they were all written, the days that were ordained for me, when as yet there was not one of them" (Psalm 139:13-16).

So listen my friend, what I say is true
  That He knew me and He knew you
He knew you then, He knows you now
  And He loves you.

He loves us and He has demonstrated His love dramatically on the cross.

"But God demonstrates His own love toward us, in that while we were yet sinners, Christ died for us. Much more then, having now been justified by His blood, we shall be saved from the wrath of God through Him" (Romans 5:8-9).

He knew you then, He knows you now
  And He died for you
He loved you then and He loves you now
  Oh I know it's true
He saw your face, He knew the place
  That you would be today
He knew you then, He knows you now
  And He loves you
He knew us then, He knows us now
    And He loves us still somehow.

That is the message of the Gospel; so simple a child could understand and yet as profound as eternity itself.

"For while we were still helpless, at the right time Christ died for the ungodly" (Romans 5:6).

THROUGH THE FLAME

It seems that often times one of the earliest lessons we try to teach our children is, "don't play with fire!" We probably especially emphasize this bit of warning because first of all, our parents gave us these same strict instructions. Secondly, we likely in many cases didn't heed the warning and discovered for ourselves that flames can scorch and fire can burn.

I remember once when I was about ten years old, I had been invited to a friend of the family's house to help rake and burn leaves during the autumn season. I don't think I was too keen on the raking part, but the opportunity to light fires and burn leaves had a great appeal to me.

The fall season, cooler weather, and the smell of piles of leaves burning, all served as a great attractant to a ten year old boy who otherwise might go play ball in the park on a brisk Saturday morning.

I loved to play baseball when I was a kid. My neighborhood friend, Butch, and I would play catch and practice our batting and out fielding skills with endless games of "500." However, as fun as all that was, I knew a fire would not break out in our imaginary World Series sessions. Perhaps one day we would develop our pitching skills to the point of "throwin heat," but at the age of ten, that was only a distant dream.

So on this particular Saturday I chose raking and burning over pitching and catching. My parents drove me to their friend Don's house down on Grey Cloud Island. I was used to raking, or at least watching others rake leaves into piles, then lighting them on fire and managing the burning pile by standing guard with a rake, and occasionally sweeping the burning leaves closer together so all would eventually be incinerated.

Don, however, had a better idea. I guess to avoid the standing guard part and the burned areas that always existed after the leaf piles had burned out, a fifty gallon drum was Don's weapon of choice to battle the ever falling leaves.

We still had to rake; but instead of loose piles to attend, we just gathered up all the leaves and mashed them down into the barrel.

After the barrel was stuffed and packed down completely with autumn's residue, the fire would be lit. I guess Don thought I was old enough or perhaps thought I'd had some previous experience in this method of botanical arson. As an elder would pass some priceless treasure to an eager youth, Don passed a box of matches to me.

He gave me that look that says, "I know you know what to do with these." I knew what they were, how they worked and what they could do, but I didn't know exactly what he wanted me to do with them.

I didn't know, that is until he told me, "Pour a little of the gas in that can over there onto the leaves in the barrel and light it."

I should say here, "a little gas" is a relative term. As Don turned to rake more leaves on the ground, I turned to pour "a little gas" on the leaves in the barrel. It didn't seem like a lot to me. There was still some left in the can, though probably not as much as Don would have preferred.

Yes, I lit the match while standing directly next to the barrel, even looking down in to insure ignition.

I didn't remain standing long, however, as the barrel suddenly resembled one of those old Civil War mortar cannons. Webster defines a mortar as follows: "A muzzle-loading cannon having a tube short in relation to its caliber that is used to throw projectiles with low muzzle velocities at high angles."

What a perfect definition of what happened! Muzzle loaded, leaves packed in from the top. A short tube. Yes, a fifty gallon drum is a short tube compared to its wide diameter. "Projectiles with low muzzle velocities at high angles" is an absolutely perfect description of what I witnessed as thousands of leaves blew heavenward at a mostly vertical angle!

To witness this all while lying flat on the ground is a memory still clear in my mind. I also clearly remember Don running over, looking down at me and asking if I was OK. I then noticed he had a rather puzzled look come across his face.

I guess he'd never seen a ten year old boy with the front part of his hair and all of his eye brows completely singed off.

I must have appeared to him as some sort of other-worldly alien.

It's interesting to observe here that as Christians we are viewed by the world in similar fashion.

We are on a journey in a foreign land
  Weary pilgrims trying to find our way
We really don't belong here, we're just passing through
  We're all looking for a brighter day.

It's kind of like that old song that goes, "This world is not my home, I'm just a passin through."

Scripture refers to us as aliens, foreigners, sojourners and pilgrims. We live in this world but we're really not of this world. That Saturday morning many years ago, as I lay on the ground, I'm sure there was a different look on my face as I had just endured a great epiphany.

Perhaps there was a glow on my face, both from the surprise and the heat. As true Christians with an eternal perspective we live in the glow of a great epiphany as well.

"Therefore if any man is in Christ, he is a new creature; the old things passed away; behold, new things have come" (2 Corinthians 5:17).

We now live life with a view to the eternal.

One day we'll see Jesus, look upon His face
When we stand before Him on that day
We will sing His praises, shout His name on high
With the host of Heaven we will say

Through the flame through the fire
Through the storm through the flood
We have been lifted higher
By the strength, by the blood of the Lamb.

"When you pass through the waters, I will be with you; and through the rivers, they will not overflow you. When you walk through the fire, you will not be scorched, nor will the flame burn you" (Isaiah 43:2).

It's important to note that this verse says, "*when you pass through...*" not, if you pass through.

Scripture assures us that we will be tested and tried. The imagery that Scripture uses of flames and floods, speaks to us of powerful if not devastating forces. At the same time Scripture teaches us that fire and water are both refining and cleansing agents.

One of my favorite stories in the Bible is that of Shadrach, Meshach and Abednego.

We know from Scripture these were three good looking smart young men: "*...youths in whom was no defect, who were good looking, showing intelligence in every branch of wisdom, endowed with understanding...*" *(Daniel 1:4).*

One day King Nebuchadnezzar builds a golden image to himself which was roughly ninety feet tall by nine feet wide.

You know the story; the King announces to all the leaders, all the "movers and shakers," and all the "up and comers" in the land to assemble at a given spot at a certain time.

Once all are assembled, the King tells them he's going to "strike up the band;" and when they hear the music they are to each and every one bow down and worship the golden image. And oh, by the way, "*But whoever does not fall down and worship shall immediately be cast into the midst of a furnace of blazing fire*" *(Daniel 3:6).*

This is an object lesson that really packs a punch!

The band plays, the furnace burns, and the people bow. Well not all the people. Those three smart, good looking Hebrews are still standing. Don't you know that incited some jealous rage; especially from the not-so-smart, not-so-good looking, and not-so-Hebrew, tattle-tale Chaldeans.

Of course they couldn't wait to tell the King about these dissenters and see if he would stand by his word and burn these boys!

The King orders the three Hebrew lads to be brought before him so he could repeat the drill just in case they hadn't heard or didn't understand.

Once again…the band, bow, or burn!

I love their response; *"O Nebuchadnezzar, we do not need to give you an answer concerning this matter…our God whom we serve is able to deliver us from the furnace of blazing fire; and He will deliver us out of your hand, O King, but even if He does not, let it be known to you, O King, that we are not going to serve your gods or worship the golden image that you have set up" (Daniel 3:16-18).*

Well that did it! The King blew a gasket, ordered the furnace to be heated up seven times hotter and commanded some of his valiant warriors to throw these boys into the furnace of certain death. Once I had my hair and eyebrows singed by being too close to the fire; but as these warriors came close to the furnace to deposit their defyers, they literally had a "melt down" and perished.

Shadrach, Meshach and Abednego were thrown in fully clothed and bound.

Through some tribulations, through the tempter's snares
 Always with our foe on every side
We kept pressing onward to a promised land
 Often as by fire we were tried.

Suddenly, to the King's utter amazement, he looked into the furnace and saw what appeared to be four men walking around.

"Look! I see four men loosed and walking about in the midst of the fire without harm, and the appearance of the fourth is like a son of the gods!" (Daniel 3:25).

The King tells the three young men to, "*...come out, you servants of the Most High God...*" and they do.

Only one thing is different from the time they were thrown in until they stepped out. The fire had no effect on their bodies, nor was their hair singed or their trousers damaged and they didn't even smell like smoke.

But what about their bonds? They were thrown in tied up, but the King said he saw them loosed and walking around in the fire.

They found freedom in the fire! That fourth one, who appeared as a son of the gods, was in fact the Son of God!

He could have delivered them from the fire then just as He could deliver us from the fires of affliction and adversity now. But He knows that often, if not usually, it's a more precious and valuable lesson to be delivered Through the Flame.

Soon it will be over, never more to roam
  As our weary souls to Him we bring
Laying down our sorrows, lifting up our praise
  To the Rock of Ages we will sing.

"Beloved, do not be surprised at the fiery ordeal among you, which comes upon you for your testing, as though some strange thing were happening to you; but to the degree that you share the sufferings of Christ, keep on rejoicing; so that at the revelation of His glory, you may rejoice with exultation" (1 Peter 4:12-13).

WAITING

Can't see the light at the end of the tunnel
  Can't see that far down the road
Waiting in darkness I'm tempted to stumble
  Weary from bearing this load
Desperately weighing all of my options
  Scheming to find my own way
But after all of my planning is over
  This is the most I can say
Lord I'm waiting…

From a song crafting point of view, this is one of my favorite songs of all that I have written. I love the imagery, the poetry and the melody. It's one of my favorite songs to play on the guitar. The chord structure is both challenging, at least for me, and musically gratifying when played well.

Its theme is universal. We have all waited for someone or something.

I could go on about this song as to what I like about it, but what I don't like about it is I can't remember where, when or why I wrote it!

As I was looking back through my discography I was surprised to discover I had written it in 1986 or thereabouts.

It first appeared on an album entitled, "Against The Wind", which was released in 1986. As I reflected on the lyrics of the title song on that recording I gained some insight.

Problems on the rise, troubles just increase
  Responsibilities never cease
Fears and doubts assail, worries from within
  Sometimes life is just like walking against the wind.

I do remember that this was one of my last recordings to be available on either 33 1/3 lp record, cassette and CD.

Technology was changing once again. I had lived through such changes before. In 1966 I recorded my first album on monaural vinyl. My next record was also on vinyl, but it was stereo. At that same time, 45's were used to play my singles at radio stations. Then came 8-track cartridges followed soon after by cassettes. There was rumored talk of a new format called a CD. All I'd ever heard of a CD was as a certificate of deposit at the bank for investment purposes.

My parents, who never had a lot of money, did purchase some CD's at the bank when interest rates were about 18%. I guess those were the good old days, at least if you were investing, not borrowing!

However, the CD's I was hearing about in the recording industry sounded like they were going to look sort of like small, shiny, chrome records. And they would be sonically superior to anything we had previously heard because they were digital (whatever that was).

A time of significant transition was coming. It was coming not only to technology, but in 1986 it was coming to my life.

As I have shared elsewhere, 1987 was to be a significant time of change and challenge. Dallas Holm and Praise would disband and my wife, Linda, would be diagnosed with cancer.

I had no specific indication of the changes that lay just ahead, but I remember I had a sense of change coming.

I look back now, even in reading the lyrics for, "Waiting," and am so thankful to God that He was preparing me for what was to come.

He was mercifully and patiently teaching me one of His most valuable lessons in life….waiting!

"Wait for the Lord; Be strong, and let your heart take courage; Yes, wait for the Lord" (Psalm 27:14).

Lord I'm waiting Lord I'm waiting
And I'm not going to move
Till I'm able to prove Your will
Lord I'm waiting Lord I'm waiting
Listening for You with my heart.

"The majority of us know nothing about waiting, we don't wait, we endure. Waiting means that we go on in the perfect certainty of God's goodness." (Oswald Chambers).

Waiting is not laziness or even passivity, though I suppose, ill-regarded, it could be thought to be so.

Waiting on the Lord or waiting for the Lord are intentionally purposed actions designed to sense the Lord's leading, perchance to hear His still small voice.

Though this kind of waiting may demand a season of inactivity to gain the desired spiritual goal, it is none the less an action taken which will have an equal and opposite reaction.

That equal and opposite reaction will almost always come as an onslaught of *"the cares of life,"* the *"deceitfulness of riches,"* the *"lust of the flesh,"* and *"the pride of life,"* all of which Scripture warns.

As worries, distractions, and pressures mount, we are tempted to abandon our "waiting period" before the Lord and seek to re-establish some sense of momentum to our lives.

However, our best efforts to get ourselves back on track and moving forward will be to our own peril if we are moving when He is telling us to wait.

It is so much easier to entertain the seemingly brilliant thoughts of our minds than to *"Be still and know that He is God" (Psalm 46:10).* Some translations say: *"Cease striving and know that I am God."* I like that!

We know from Scripture that,

"My thoughts are not your thoughts, neither are your ways My ways… for as the heavens are higher than the earth, so are My ways higher than your ways, and My thoughts than your thoughts" (Isaiah 55:8-9).

Still, we consider our options sometimes because: *"There is a way which seems right to a man…" (Proverbs 14:12).*

Lord it's so easy to find a solution
  Something that seems right to me
But plans that are born out of my own confusion
  Will not help my blind eyes to see.

Proverbs 14:12 concludes by saying, "*…but its end is the way of death.*"

Walking in our ways, derived from confusion and blindness, never ends well. Walking in His ways always ends well.

"The steps of a good man are established by the Lord; and He delights in his way. When he falls, he shall not be hurled headlong; because the Lord is the One who holds his hand" (Psalm 37:23-24).

Matthew Henry, the great commentator said this, "Observe, God orders the steps of a good man; not only His way in general, by His written Word, but by His particular steps, by the whispers of conscience, saying, 'This is the way, walk in it.' He does not always show him His way at a distance, but leads him step by step, as children are led, and so keeps him in a continual dependence upon His guidance."

All of the steps that You've layed out before me
  Steps that are Yours and not mine
So I'll be content just to wait in Your presence
  Patiently biding Your time.

I love that last line, "...biding Your time!" This is what we must come to realize in all of our life; it's His time. Our lives are His. Our time is His. And truth be known, sometimes when we think we're waiting on Him, He's actually waiting on us!

"Therefore the Lord longs to be gracious to you, and therefore He waits on high to have compassion on you" (Isaiah 30:18).

Lord I have need of patience
    Help me to rest in you
I am detained in my weakness
    There's not a thing I can do

"Patience is the result of well-centered strength. To 'wait on the Lord,' and to 'rest in the Lord' is an indication of a healthy, holy faith, while impatience is an indication of an un-healthy, un-holy unbelief." (Oswald Chambers)

So Lord I'm waiting Lord I'm waiting
    And I'm not going to move
Till I'm able to prove Your will
    Lord I'm waiting Lord I'm waiting
Listening for You with my heart.

Are you in a waiting period just now? Does it seem as though time has slowed and your patience is running out? Have you conjured up within your mind plans and schemes that would seem sensible to your idea of reason and logic?

May I encourage you this moment to continue to wait on the Lord. Waiting for His will is so much to be preferred over moving in your strength.

The old saying goes, "Anything worthwhile is worth waiting for." Interesting that even the world knows this to be true. Yet, sometimes we as Christians lose sight of the fact that God's best plans and purposes are often realized through waiting.

"Lead me in Thy truth and teach me, for Thou art the God of my salvation; For Thee I wait all the day" (Psalm 25:5).

BEFORE YOUR THRONE

It seems I've always had somewhat of an overactive imagination. I can remember as a boy always imagining I was someone else or somewhere else. It wasn't that I was at odds with who I was or where I lived; but to be me, with perhaps the ability to fly or run faster than a speeding bullet, captured my imagination.

I suppose that a daily dose of the old black and white Superman TV show, that aired after I got home from school, served to heighten my fantasies.

I loved where I grew up in St. Paul Park, Minnesota. It was a small town located about ten miles south of the capital city of St. Paul.

Situated right by the Mississippi River, it was nearly perfect for a boy who was born with a huge love of the outdoors and all things related to nature.

Often I would ride my 24" balloon tire Schwinn bike down to Grey Cloud Island to pursue a day of adventure in the woods or on the water.

Grey Cloud Island had a rich history dating back to early Native American Woodland mound-builders (100 B.C. to 600 A.D.) and for people of the Late Mississippian culture around 1000 A.D.

Needless-to-say, my bike was a horse and I was an Indian, as I would set off into the unknown wilderness of my native ancestors.

My Uncle Ray lived on a slough that acted as a sort of moat to encircle and protect the 2,000 acre island and its 200 or so residents. He had a canoe which was mine to use whenever I wanted, providing I took care of it and, "put it back exactly as you found it."

Often I would paddle up the slough, spearing carp or garfish and occasionally catching a snapping turtle. Of course, I always had to be cautious and vigilant because warring hostile tribes could be lurking in the reeds and cat-tails, just out of sight, waiting to pounce and capture or kill a young brave like myself.

It never happened, but I imagined it could!

The imaginings of a boy ultimately fade into reality. As a boy, I often dreaded bedtime, for I knew it was then that my imagination would take a dark turn and the daydreams would become nightmares.

Alas, adulthood has negated the nightmares; and the serene sleep of the senior season of life is my portion, though still often accompanied by dreams, and in living color!

This brings me to the song, "Before Your Throne." It was inspired by a dream. Now before you roll your eyes and dismiss me as one of those "dream tellers," let me explain.

In the mid-nineties I was ministering at a church where many were being saved and God was moving in a powerful way. One night I had a dream. In the dream I saw the sanctuary and out of the inner walls of the sanctuary water was flowing. It cascaded out from the walls as some beautiful four-sided fountain and flowed down to the floor where it began to rise, getting deeper and deeper.

In the dream I seemed to know that the water represented some aspect of the glory of God. That was it…end of dream!

I make no claims that God gave me that dream. I don't know, though Scripture does say, *"Your old men will dream dreams, your young men will see visions" (Joel 2:28).*

This Scripture is revisited in the New Testament: *"AND IT SHALL BE IN THE LAST DAYS, GOD SAYS, THAT I WILL POUR FORTH OF MY SPIRIT UPON ALL MANKIND…AND YOUR YOUNG MEN SHALL SEE VISIONS, AND YOUR OLD MEN SHALL DREAM DREAMS" (Acts 2:17).*

At this point in my life I'm not sure if I fall into the category of young men or old men. It doesn't really matter because again, I make no claims to have had a dream or vision from God.

I was, however, influenced and I believe inspired to write a song about the glory of God in the presence of His throne room.

I suppose my imagination suited me well for science fiction, and that's probably why Twilight Zone was a favorite program of mine. It often explored the realm of parallel universes, which I always found a fascinating concept.

Just recently I watched a documentary where several couples were brought together who looked absolutely like identical twins but shared no common ancestry, national origins or even DNA.

Very interesting, yet in no way supporting any kind of parallel universe theory. Just every once in a while, some people look alike. That's it!

But in considering the Throne of God, I am struck with the fact that though God is on His Throne…somewhere, still He invites me to come into His presence.

We know from Scripture that after Jesus' life and ministry on earth, He ascended into Heaven. *"So then, when the Lord had spoken to them, He was received up into Heaven, and sat down at the right hand of God" (Mark 16:19).*

In the book of Acts, the ascension account reads as follows: *"And after He had said these things, He was lifted up while they were looking on, and a cloud received Him out of their sight. And as they were gazing intently into the sky while He was departing, behold, two men in white clothing stood beside them; and they also said, 'Men of Galilee, why do you stand looking into the sky? This Jesus, who has been taken up from you into Heaven, will come in just the same way as you have watched Him go into Heaven!'" (Acts 1:9-11).*

The early Christians who would have read these words would surely conclude, as we do today, that Jesus was taken up, away, and our assumption would most likely be, taken far away.

Yet Scripture says, *"Let us go into His dwelling place; let us worship at His footstool" (Psalm 132:7).*

"Let us go" would suggest that we need to make a move or go to some other place. Can we travel to Heaven? As Christians, some day we will, but not yet.

Is this some kind of spiritual parallel universe dilemma? Let's look at the second part of that verse to get an answer.

"Let us worship at His footstool." OK, where is that? *"Heaven is My Throne, and the earth is My footstool" (Isaiah 66:1).*

So, though His Throne is in Heaven, He gives us the imagery that His feet rest upon the earth, *"His footstool."*

This is a big God! And He is, to be sure!

Perhaps the greatest reason our worship is often stunted and small is that we have not a big enough image of God. His heights are higher than the heavens, His depths, deeper than the oceans and His love is beyond our ability to express.

There is a higher place than I have ever been
There is a deeper well than I can comprehend
There is a greater love than I have ever known
And it's here, yes it's here, Lord it's here
Before Your Throne.

There is a greater mercy than man could ere conceive
There is a stronger faith than we would dare believe
There is a place of rest where we'll never feel alone
And it's here, yes it's here, Lord it's here
Before Your Throne.

So I bow down before You and cry holy
Lord I fall at Your feet and praise Your name
I am bathed in the light of Your glory
And it's here, yes it's here, Lord it's here
Before Your Throne.

"Exalt the Lord our God, and worship at His footstool; Holy is He" (Psalm 99:5).

So here we are on planet earth and God is in Heaven, but He invites us to "*go into His dwelling place.*"

How then is this accomplished? How is anything accomplished within the realm of our relationship to God? Faith!

We are saved by grace through faith, we are justified by faith, we walk by faith and we pray in faith. *"Without faith it is impossible to please God" (Hebrews 11:6).*

So by faith, we believe we come into the very throne room of God through worship, praise and petition.

By faith, we believe there is forgiveness of sin, healing for life's woundings and light for those who walk in darkness.

Do you this day need forgiveness of sin? Does your heart and perhaps your body need the touch of the Great Physician? And is there someone for whom you are praying who has yet to see the Light of the World?

There are rivers of forgiveness to cleanse the soul from sin
    There healing waters flowing to heal the wounds within
There's a light of pure redemption to lead the wayward home
    And it's here, yes it's here, Lord it's here
Before Your Throne.

"And I looked, and I heard the voice of many angels around the Throne and the living creatures and the elders; and the number of them was myriads of myriads, and thousands of thousands, saying with a loud voice, 'Worthy is the Lamb that was slain to receive power and riches and wisdom and might and honor and glory and blessing.' And every created thing which is in heaven and on the earth and under the sea, and all things in them, I heard saying, 'To Him who sits on the Throne, and to the Lamb, be blessing and honor and glory and dominion forever and ever'" (Revelation 5:11-13)

STRENGTH

I guess all little boys are impressed by muscles and strength. I know I was. My uncle, whose name was Clarence (though we all called him Kise), was an impressive figure of a man. Uncle Kise got his name from my Mom, who as a little girl, the youngest of five children, was unable to clearly say Clarence. She tried, but it always came out sounding like Kise and so that name stuck throughout his life.

Uncle Kise was a unique individual, to say the least. He was an amazing fisherman, hunter, trapper and probably the most knowledgeable and experienced outdoorsman I've ever known.

He taught me how to shoot and how to hunt. He taught me to love and respect God's creation, though I think the love of nature was born in me. We had numerous adventures in the woods and on the water, beginning in my childhood and lasting well into my adult years.

He was a man of few words; but on occasion, like once when we were ice fishing on a Mississippi River slough, he broke the silence with:

God grant that I may live to fish
Until my dying day,
And when it comes to my last cast,
I then most humbly pray,
When in the Lord's safe landing net,
I'm peacefully asleep,
That in His mercy I be judged,
As big enough to keep.
(Author Unknown)

I loved our times together though few words were spoken. Quite frankly, sometimes words clutter the lines of communication that exist firmly between kindred souls.

I was impressed by how he could ride a bicycle backwards, sitting on the handle bars facing rearward and pedaling in reverse. Uncle Kise could walk down a flight of stairs…on his hands! Impressive!

He often hunted squirrels, rabbits, and pheasants with a slingshot, providing many a meal for his family in so doing.

The list goes on and on, but you get the picture…"one of a kind," "broke the mold," "rugged individual", etc.

But of all the things that impressed me, especially as a young boy, it was his physical strength, athletic ability and physique that impressed me most. Nowadays we would say, he was "ripped!"

I can remember as a young boy looking at myself in the mirror, flexing my little biceps and wondering if I would ever have muscles like Uncle Kise. I'd go to the refrigerator, open the door and pull out that box of Arm and Hammer baking soda, place it on the counter and wonder what a guy had do to get an arm like the one on that product's logo.

Once when I was probably about six or seven, I was standing in our bathroom, resplendent in my Jockey shorts, flexing my skinny little arms in the mirror, trying desperately to see anything that might resemble a muscle.

Just then my Mom walked by, knew exactly what was going on and, rather than embarrass me, she praised me for my big muscles. I think she had glasses on and apparently could see things I couldn't.

To further encourage me, she got her camera and said, "Let's go outside where the light is good and I'll take a picture of you."

I was quite a shy young boy, and standing out in the yard in front of our house in my "tighty whities" was not something I had previously contemplated.

As it was a small town and the middle of the day, she convinced me it was highly unlikely anyone would be driving by. A few cars at 5:00 or so was the normal rush hour on Portland Ave.

So I walked out the front door reluctantly and struck my pose, which was kind of a cross between Charles Atlas and Superman getting ready to "leap a tall building in a single bound."

And just as Mom snapped the picture, an eighteen wheeler came down our street and honked his air horn, just in case anyone in the entire county was missing this photo shoot.

I'd never seen a big truck on our street prior to that and I think perhaps one has not appeared since. I guess miracles are exciting, but that one...not so much!

Recently I ran across that photo. I wish I could show it to you, but I would still be embarrassed. As I studied the photo I smiled, remembering all the circumstances that surrounded that moment. It seemed so long ago and I guess it was, at least over sixty years now.

Between then and now I reached my prime, at least physically. To prepare for various adventures in the wild and in an attempt to stay fit for life's challenges, I did achieve the muscles and strength I longed for as a boy.

I've noticed though that time and gravity seem to eventually win out over our best efforts.

Uncle Kise has been gone for a number of years now. I was blessed to talk with him on the phone only hours before he passed. I assured him that where he was going, there would be taller mountains, cleaner rivers and bigger fish! His last words to me were, "I'll be lookin for ya." And I know he will.

This may all seem a strange and perhaps even somewhat silly recounting of days past. But I believe to some degree it encapsulates the journey of us all.

If we've lived for any significant amount of time on earth, we've each likely experienced the physical challenges and eventual diminishment that accompanies our life's journey. If we haven't as yet experienced this reality in our own lives and bodies, we've undoubtedly witnessed its effects in others.

But I don't think it's the physical realm that most challenges our efforts if not even our faith at times. It's the feelings of hopelessness - the mental and emotional anguish that the world, the flesh and the devil throw our way in an attempt to diminish and attack our faith, our hope and our strength.

Sometimes this life can get confusing
  Sometimes the days can seem so long
I'm trying to win but feel I'm losing
  I'm doing right but feeling wrong.

I've felt this way at times, have you? Have others? David, "a man after God's own heart," did.

"How long, O Lord? Wilt Thou forget me forever? How long wilt Thou hide Thy face from me? How long shall I take counsel in my soul, having sorrow in my heart all the day? How long will my enemy be exalted over me?" (Psalm 13:1-2).

This is the same David who had previously written, *"O Lord, our Lord, How majestic is Thy name in all the earth" (Psalm 8:1).*

"I will give thanks to the Lord with all my heart; I will tell of all Thy wonders. I will be glad and exult in Thee; I will sing praise to Thy name, O Most High" (Psalm 9:1-2).

So David questions whether the Lord will forget him, yet he extols the majesty of His name. He feels God has hidden His face from him, yet he vows to sing praises to the name of the Lord.

Don't David's words typify the turbulence often found in all our lives?

I need a power that is greater
  I need a faith to keep me strong
I need a love to give me courage
  I need a Savior who can guide me through the storm.

I need strength to hold on to You
  I need strength to know what to do
I need strength just to make it through the day
  I need strength just to hold Your hand
I need strength just to make a stand
  I need strength just to know Your plan for me.

This song is a prayer as well as an affirmation that we need the strength of the Lord for every aspect of our lives.

"Hear the voice of my supplications when I cry to Thee for help…" (Psalm 28:2).

I want you in my life completely
  All that I need You give by grace
When life is hard You come so sweetly
  And give me strength to run the race.

"The Lord is my strength and my shield; My heart trusts in Him, and I am helped;

Therefore my heart exults, and with my song I shall thank Him" (Psalm 28:7).

In my weakness Your strength is made
  Perfect in me
When I feel I can't go on
  Your power, Your power is all I need.

When we pray for strength we can always be assured that God will faithfully answer. However, He may answer in ways other than what we might anticipate. We ask for strength with a certain expectation of what that will look like. But if *"In our weakness His strength is perfected,"* might it not follow that the answer to our prayer may very well be the diminishment if not removal of things we might deem as strength? And then in our weakness we shall learn to rely on Him completely. Then we will sing:

Your power, Your power is <u>all</u> I need!

I need strength just to feel Your grace
  I need strength just to keep Your pace
I need strength just to run the race for You
  I need strength just to stand the test
I need strength just to do my best
  I need strength just to find my rest in You.

"I love Thee, O Lord, my strength. The Lord is my rock and my fortress and my deliverer. My God, my rock, in whom I take refuge; My shield and the horn of my salvation, my stronghold" (Psalm 18;1-2).

THE GOOD SAMARITAN

Beaten weary left along the way
  Dry from thirst til word I could not say
Then you came walking by and looked into my eye
  Saw my need and stopped to rescue me.

"A certain man was going down from Jerusalem to Jericho; and he fell among robbers, and they stripped him and beat him, and went off leaving him half dead. And by chance a certain priest was going down on that road, and when he saw him, he passed by on the other side. And likewise a Levite also, when he came to the place and saw him, passed by on the other side.

But a certain Samaritan, who was on a journey, came upon him; and when he saw him, he felt compassion, and came to him, and bandaged up his wounds, pouring oil and wine on them; and he put him on his own beast, and brought him to an inn, and took care of him.

And on the next day he took out two denarii and gave them to the innkeeper and said, 'Take care of him; and whatever more you spend, when I return, I will repay you.'

Which of these three do you think proved to be a neighbor to the man who fell into the robbers' hands?" (Luke 10:30-36).

This story from Luke's Gospel has always been one of my favorite parables; so much so that early in my Christian walk I wrote a song entitled, "The Good Samaritan."

Though this is one of my earliest Christian songs, written probably at the age of 18 or 19, it remains to this day one of my personal favorites.

My earliest remembrance of this parable is as a five or six year old boy sitting in a Sunday School class. The story was taught to this class of little boys and girls by means of the universal Bible story-telling technology known as the flannel board.

Now if you don't know what I'm talking about I'll try my best to describe it. The flannel board was about the size of an average painting. It was in fact a piece of art which usually sat upon an A-frame easel as you would display any noteworthy artistic rendering. The flannel board, however, was usually of a little more generic depiction.

A landscape, perhaps with a mountain, some trees and a road would serve as a back drop to the central focal points which would be added.

The main components of this evolving work of art would be little cut out figures of Bible characters, animals, Noah's ark or any number of other items, also made of flannel, to complete the masterpiece and teach the Bible story.

The nature of the flannel fabric used on both the board and the cut outs caused the Bible characters, animals or props to adhere to the board. Static electricity was also helpful.

Thus, a piece of art, sure to capture the minds of "the little children," could be arranged and rearranged in the process of presenting the Bible story.

There was a problem, however, unique to this technology. Sometimes static electricity gave out! Sometimes the flannel figures got worn out and smoothed off (not so unlike what happens to most of us with time and use).

Of course for me, this was the point in every Bible story I hoped for – some holy figure from the Old Testament starting to slip a little, or the thought of that angel hovering over the manger suddenly detaching and diving to the linoleum floor. I would stifle the laughter welling up within me from my overactive imagination. I was well aware that, for the most part, the laughter of little children or anyone for that matter, seemed to have no place within the walls of the "sanctuary of the solemn."

Though never specifically taught, every child knew the four major "kid's commandments."

1. Sit up straight
2. Pay attention
3. Don't talk
4. Don't run

I remember one particular Sunday when a flannel Moses began to peel off from the board, finally fully letting go and gently drifting down, as a detached autumn leaf, to the hard floor beneath the flannel board.

There was a moment of silence; however it was only a moment, followed by an explosion of little boys and girls laughing as Moses ultimately came to rest beneath the teacher's foot.

For us it was a wonderful moment. For the teacher, who was not aware that Moses had taken flight and came to rest beneath her all-seeing eye, it was an opportunity to once again remind us of a couple of the kids' commandments.

How could anyone miss the humor of a man who can make it through the Red Sea but can't stick on the flannel board?

Once, while we were being taught the story of the Good Samaritan, I realized something else that was not so much humorous as it was interesting, if not perplexing.

The teacher told us of a man who was one day walking down a road, only to be set upon by robbers, beaten, and left to die in the ditch. As she placed the little flannel Bible guy in the ditch, I noticed he looked a lot like Joseph. In fact he looked exactly like Joseph; same yellow robe, beard and long hair as in the Christmas story.

As the three other characters in the story arrived on the scene and eventually departed, I sensed a strong familiarity with them as well.

Maybe because the priest, the Levite and the Samaritan in this presentation were carrying gold, frankincense and myrrh.

Where had I seen these guys before?

I now believe we probably had some budget issues at that very small church. We apparently couldn't afford the complete deluxe set of Bible characters, so our small company of flannel actors and actresses played many varied roles in their weekly performances.

For example, many months after the Good Samaritan presentation, I was sure I was seeing the same characters, but in an altogether different story from a different time period.

I was pretty sure that as Shadrach, Meshach and Abednego were going into the flannel furnace, they were carrying with them gold, frankincense and myrrh. The little guy standing next to the furnace, playing the part of King Nebuchadnezzar (though he looked kinda like Jonah), said, *"Did not we throw three men into the furnace? But I see a fourth and he appears to be as a son of the gods?"* Well I leaned forward in my little chair, looked in and thought to myself, "No...pretty sure that's Joseph!"

All in all I consider myself blessed to have been exposed to such multi-talented actors who week after week came out of their little maroon colored cigar box to teach the great stories of the Bible.

The cigar box was a distraction for me because my Dad had told my brother and me in no uncertain terms that he didn't want to ever catch us smoking.

So which of the saints among us had smoked all those cigars I wondered. Was it our Sunday School teacher, a tall stately woman who seemed to embody the very essence of holiness? I don't think so. Must have been someone else who if questioned about it would probably respond with, "I was just making room for the Bible characters."

I guess it doesn't really matter. What does matter is that I remember all those stories. I could tell you where I was sitting the day I learned the story of the Good Samaritan. Second row, one seat from the end, next to a little girl named Sharon.

I got the point of the story! Be like that third guy! See the needs that may exist around you that others don't see or don't want to involve themselves in.

In over four decades of ministry I've become involved in the lives of many; literally rescuing them from certain death by presenting the Gospel message of salvation and hope by God's grace through faith.

And so it was a story well taught, with some little flannel Bible characters that lived in a maroon colored cigar box a long, long time ago.

As I've often said, when we read the Bible we find God and we find ourselves. Where are you, or more precisely, who are you in this story?

Are you perhaps as that one beaten and left along the way? Maybe you've not been set upon by robbers, but life has dealt significant blows! Have the *"cares of life"* almost overwhelmed you? And to add insult to injury, there are those around you who should care but don't seem to. You need help but they seem disinclined as did the priest and the Levite. Does it seem the world, the flesh and the devil have all conspired to strip you bare and leave you half dead?

Others came and others went on by
  Refused to help or just too tired to try
Alone at last I sat, my head fell slowly back
  And words from deep within me reached the sky.

I'm hungry please feed me
  I'm naked please clothe me
I'm so alone, won't someone come to me
  The sound of my words died
Oh well, at least I tried
  And trying seemed the only thing to do.

Remember that the reason we are given the parable of the Good Samaritan is because *"…a certain lawyer stood up and put Him (Jesus) to the test, saying, 'Teacher, what shall I do to inherit eternal life?'"* Jesus responds by asking the lawyer what the Law states. Of course, Jesus knows the lawyer knew full well the text of the Law.

The lawyer responds: *"You shall love the Lord your God with all your heart, and with all your soul, and with all your strength, and with all your mind; and your neighbor as yourself" (Luke 10:25-27).*

This text is remarkable! It highlights four ways in which we are to love the Lord - with our heart, soul, strength and mind. In other words with every capacity of our created being! Then He adds to this one more thing of equal importance, "…*and your neighbor as yourself.*"

Remember, these are the requirements for inheriting eternal life! These are not mere suggestions of "how to become a better you."

From the authority of Scripture I can assure you God is faithful, His grace is sufficient, He is touched with the feelings of our infirmities. He looks to those with a broken heart and a contrite spirit, and He is a very present help in our time of need.

Sometimes He will send one, as that Good Samaritan, who you do not even know; but send someone, He will. The Lord Himself will always be to you that One who rescues and saves.

He will bandage you, pour His oil upon you, carry you to safety and pay your debt.

Be encouraged, but remember also, there are those around you who have similarly been beaten and left for dead.

Has someone He sent shown up just in time for your rescue? Will you too be that *"neighbor"* to rescue others? Don't be as those who *"went on by,"* but be that one who stops to help, heal and save.

Speak the words of Jesus to those who feel valueless and forgotten: *"Are not five sparrows sold for two cents? And yet not one of them is forgotten before God... Do not fear, you are of more value than many sparrows" (Luke 12:6-7).*

But no sooner had I stopped and you were there
 And then I knew that God had heard my prayer
I should have realized and not have been surprised
 His eye is on the sparrow so why not me.

"Let us therefore draw near with confidence to the throne of grace, that we may receive mercy and may find grace to help in time of need" (Hebrews 4:16).

RISE AGAIN

Of all the songs I've written through the years, "Rise Again" is probably my best known. From a pure song crafting point of view, I'm not sure I would place this as my best lyrical and musical presentation.

It's so simple with little variation either in theme or melody, yet God seemed to inspire it, form it and oversee every aspect of its impact throughout the life of the song.

I can hardly believe it's been 40 years since I wrote "Rise Again." To give some context, I was ministering with David Wilkerson in 1976 when I wrote the song. David is best known for his book, "The Cross and The Switchblade," which chronicles the journey of a country preacher from Pennsylvania who in the late 50's felt called to go and reach the gangs and drug addicts in New York City with the message of the Gospel.

In the 60's, drugs began to spread out of the cities into smaller towns and even the remotest rural settings. David felt God's call to develop a crusade-style ministry to bring the message of the Gospel to the youth culture in America as well as abroad.

In 1969 while serving as youth pastor at a church in Ft. Worth, Texas, I received a phone call one evening from David Wilkerson.

At the time, he was ministering in an outreach in Eugene, Oregon. He was coming to a church in the Dallas area in a few weeks; and having heard one of my early recordings, he asked if I might come to his meeting in Dallas and sing a couple songs.

To make a long story shorter, I sang, we talked and prayed and he invited me to join his crusade team. This initial meeting was in October of 1969. In December of that year I resigned my position at the church, drove to Minnesota and married my fiancée, Linda Satterberg. By the first of January, 1970, we were in New York to begin our life together as well as our ministry with David Wilkerson.

I proceeded to travel and minister with Bro. Dave (as we all called him) for the next 10 ½ years. We traveled everywhere in the United States and many countries abroad, ministering to thousands of people nightly in the crusade services.

By the mid 70's we were finding ourselves ministering more and more on college campuses, on the beaches of both east and west coasts during spring breaks and in various unique venues. Always the young people showed up; Christians, non-Christians, hippies, The Black Panthers, Brown Berets and just about every representation of the youth culture you could imagine!

As a result, in 1976, Bro. Dave suggested that perhaps a band would be a more effective way to reach this ever-diversifying audience. For six years I had been a solo artist, just me and my guitar, and it had been effective. But after much prayer and discussion, we both felt a band was a good idea.

Therefore, Dallas Holm and Praise was formed. In the process of creating this new entity, I realized I would need to write some new material. One day I sat down with pencil and tablet and tried to come up with some new lyrical or musical ideas. This had generally not been a difficult process; and in fact, some of my better songs had come through just getting out the pencil and paper and working hard.

However, this particular day…nothing! Not one idea came to mind, not even a note upon which to build. Frustrating! With a sense of desperation I began to pray for help and guidance.

Ever notice how desperation and frustration often lead to prostration (spiritually and literally) before a Holy God? Suddenly, through prayer, we become so keenly aware of our own inadequacies and our absolute dependence upon Him for even our thoughts.

Wouldn't we all do well to always make prayer our first response to any and every challenge? One of my favorite Scriptures is, *"Trust in the Lord with all your heart, and do not lean on your own understanding. In all your ways acknowledge Him, and He will direct your path" (Proverbs 3:5-6).*

I might paraphrase and elaborate on that verse to myself as follows: Trust with all of your heart, only and completely in the Lord, and don't depend on your own understanding, talents or abilities. Seek Him first and foremost in prayer and acknowledge Him in every way possible, and He will give you everything you need, directions for your path, words to speak and songs to sing.

I prayed, "Lord, if You were singing, what would You say?" I almost blurted it out from the frustration of the moment. It was kind of like, "C'mon, I gotta know what You would say and what You would sing."

Then in the way a young child might draw back after having expressed themselves a little too pointedly to a parent, I drew back a bit to consider what I had just asked. More importantly, the way in which I had asked was now a concern.

But God loves honesty, honest words and honest emotions. I was pretty sure He'd been asked harder questions from others down through the centuries. From Job to John, always questions and always answers.

And so God answered me that day, not in an audible voice or in lightnings and thunderings. I can't even say I heard a "still small voice", but I knew God was speaking. It was like taking dictation from some inaudible, unseen benefactor.

Go ahead drive the nails in My hands
  Laugh at Me where you stand
Go ahead, say it isn't Me
  The day will come when you will see.

The day <u>had</u> come and I <u>was</u> seeing and hearing with the eyes and ears of my heart, not my head. There was a deeper realization that it was in fact my sins that drove those nails. In the past I had doubted and I had mocked. But He loved me, saved me, called me and was now telling me in no uncertain terms what to tell other doubters and mockers.

Go ahead and mock My name
  My love for you is still the same
Go ahead and bury Me
  But very soon I will be free.

Cause I'll rise again
  Ain't no power on earth can tie Me down

Yes I'll rise again

Death can't keep Me in the ground.

"Ain't" ain't a word, or so I'd been told. I really wondered and prayed about this, although quickly because words kept coming. The word had an edge to it and perhaps would fit well on the edge of the sword that God would wield through this song to proclaim His message.

In no more than ten or fifteen minutes the song was complete. Words, music and no corrections. It was there before me, penned by my hand but delivered, I believe, from the heart and mind of God.

I've often said, "God wrote the song, I just delivered the message." "Rise Again" has touched tens of millions of lives. Testimonies through the years have assured me that many have surrendered to Jesus; and by His grace, through faith have trusted for and received from Him the gift of salvation. Many lives have been impacted in many ways through a simple song.

The purpose of my writing this account is not to impress you with the success of a song, but rather to perhaps help you learn a lesson that I've learned through this experience.

As an old song once said, "Little is much when God is in it."

"Rise Again." A simple poem, a simple melody. Some lines and notes on a page in a matter of minutes, but when breathed upon by God, eternity is impacted!

A fellow artist and song writer, Ken Medema, wrote a classic piece years ago telling the story of Moses. In the song Ken asks, "What do you hold in your hand?"

Moses held a staff, Noah held a hammer, David held a sling. I held a pencil, and most assuredly you hold something capable of life-changing impact when surrendered to, and used by, God.

So often we miss the obvious. Looking for our "15 minutes of fame," or dreaming of some great occasion to suddenly burst on the scene with our masterpiece, we lose sight of the potential we possess in the simple things.

Moses tended sheep out in the wilderness for 40 years. The staff which became the "door opener" into that whole exchange with Pharaoh was simply a tool of his trade.

Noah surely got tired of pounding pegs into the beams of an ark that was yet to see water, but the world was saved through the exercise of the tool of his trade.

David couldn't handle the armor and sword of a king, but was more than up to the task with his little sling.

Israel won the victory because of a shepherd boy with a smooth stone well placed!

You hold a staff, hammer, sling, pencil or something. You have better technology and perhaps more talent than any of the afore-mentioned.

The issue is not really the tool or the talent. The real issue is recognizing what God has placed in our hand, surrendering it completely to Him and determining to seek His glory, not ours.

I have a quote always before me on my desk. "There is no limit to what God can do with a man, providing he will not touch the glory."

Time is short; people are lost and hurting. Work while there is time and opportunity, for soon there will be neither.

Go ahead and say I'm dead and gone
  But you will see that you were wrong
Go ahead, try to hide the Son
  But all will see that I'm the One.

Cause I'll come again
  Ain't no power on earth can keep Me back
Yes I'll come again
  Come to take my people back.

"For He will be delivered to the Gentiles, and will be mocked and mistreated and spit upon, and after they have scourged Him, they will kill Him; and the third day He will rise again" (Luke 18:32-33).

AT MY WORST YOU FOUND ME

I want to share a story I received from someone just recently in regards to the song, "At My Worst You Found Me."

It reads as follows:

> Her name was Gina but I called her the Silent One. I met her at a time when society felt it necessary to identify and label severely handicapped individuals because they didn't walk, talk and read or write.
>
> Gina was one of these. She lived with her family in a home that was many miles from our school.
>
> A bus came to pick up Gina and other students daily for the long ride. Because Gina did not talk, she was unable to tell the bus driver if she needed to use a restroom; so occasionally, unfortunate and embarrassing accidents happened. This undoubtedly only added to her silent pain.
>
> When Gina became a freshman, she came to my class. I noticed in the morning the bus driver would walk her to class, holding her hand while passing other students along the way.

This upset me because I felt it must have been embarrassing to her. I explained to the driver one day that it would be OK for him to not get off the bus with Gina.

The very next day, here came Gina all by herself. Suddenly it seemed she was in her own world, not someone else's.

A teacher and I watched as she slowly made her way to class. I think it took her almost twenty minutes, as she watched the birds fly overhead and paused to look at the buildings she was passing. The sight of all the students made her smile, and when she finally reached the classroom her face literally glowed with joy and pride at the wonder and success of her brief but significant journey.

Gina soon made friends with one of our aides named Lynn. Lynn decided she wanted Gina to be a student with her in a particular studies class. This, however, would require a journey across the campus that initially would be somewhat of a challenge for Gina, especially if for some reason Lynn was not able to assist her.

Because Gina did not talk, and could not read or write, a plan was formulated in my mind to address this dilemma. It began with Lynn showing up at class to get Gina. After a few days, Lynn would wait outside the class to meet Gina and escort her to her other class.

Each day Lynn would come to meet Gina a little farther away until finally Gina was able to make the journey all by herself.

During Gina's junior year she got to be a flower girl at the graduation exercises. Dressed in a formal gown and carrying long stem roses, she joined with eleven other girls in leading the Seniors to graduation. It was fun to watch the camaraderie between all twelve girls.

Lynn then had a wonderful idea. There was a student talent show coming up and she wanted Gina to sing in it. Lynn and I knew that though Gina did not talk, she could sing. Whenever I turned the radio on she would sing. It seemed she knew every song on every station.

I sent a note home with Gina, explaining to her sister that we wanted Gina to sing in the talent show.

The next day Gina showed up with a cassette tape that had only background music on it. I put the tape into the player, the music began, Gina sang, and the voice of an angel moved the teacher and her aides to tears.

The cheerleaders voted Gina in to the show after the tryouts.

The night of the talent show arrived. Acts came and acts went. Finally a rock band played and got the audience cranked up. The crowd was noisy and Gina was next.

The curtains separated, the crowd quieted down a bit and somewhere in the audience a girl yelled, "You can do it Gina!"

Guys in front of me from the football team were making fun, and a student behind me wanted to know what kind of a joke was on stage.

Gina was sitting on a chair, a blue spotlight focused on her face. The sound track didn't start up immediately, and in that awkward silence the cheerleaders ran up and sat at her feet.

The musical intro finally started, Gina raised the microphone and began to sing:

At my worst You found me
At my worst You died
At my worst You loved me
And at my worst You tried
To tell me that the best thing I could do
Would be to give my life to You
At my worst You loved me
And now I love You too.

She had learned the song by listening to you, Dallas. You could hear people crying all over the auditorium, even the judges.

The football team was the first on their feet whistling and clapping. The rest of the crowd followed. A girl behind me told me how she had made fun of Gina in her PE class saying that "Gina was the worst."

How sorry and embarrassed she was now!

Dallas, it was the best thing that ever happened in our school. Gina didn't win the show, but she won so much more.

Two weeks later she came up to me and spoke her first words. She said, "I don't have any friends."

She did have friends at school but not at home where she lived. Apparently no one had taught her how to make friends or taken her out of the house to meet anyone.

> Her family moved away before her graduation and we were all very sad.
>
> But I wanted you to know what an impact your song had on Gina, Lynn, myself and an entire school."
>
> Sincerely,
>
> Mary

Ironically I received this story only hours before I sat down to write this chapter. Coincidence? I think not.

For our purposes here, I've changed the names of the characters in this story to protect the innocent, as they say, but the story and its details are true.

I was struck with the thought that probably all of us have known someone like Gina. Perhaps even now we know such a one as this. Maybe tomorrow we will meet or cross paths with a "Gina."

I'm reminded of a favorite quote from one of my favorite authors, Oswald Chambers. He said, "There's always one more fact in the other person's life, about which you know nothing." How sensitive we must be in the daily course of our activities to avoid saying or doing anything that might hurt or wound the already wounded.

How we should love the unlovely (according to the world's standards) as God loves them. *"Love your neighbor as yourself"* is our command as Christians. The "Ginas" of this world are our neighbors!

So many who have endured life's unfairness, who have suffered deep hurts and bitter wounds, find it difficult to believe in a God who could love them.

How could You love me Jesus
How did You know my name
Why did You save me Jesus
Oh I'll never know how You loved me so
And I'll never see what You saw in me.

We as Christians really should see our resemblance to Gina. We were all severely handicapped by sin. We were lost and continually mocked by the enemy of our soul. We were permanently disabled apart from the grace of God, and our future both in this life and beyond was nothing more than a continual downward spiral into the dark abyss. *"But God demonstrates His own love toward us, in that while we were yet sinners, Christ died for us" (Romans 5:8).*

I've always loved that Scripture! It's one of my favorites because it speaks to me of God's eternal plans and purposes for the redemption of lost souls.

Before the very foundation of the world, and most certainly before I ever drew my first breath, God made provision for my sin.

I'm reminded of an old chorus:

Oh how He loves you and me
Oh how He loves you and me
He gave His life, what more could He give
Oh how He loves you and me.

"For God so loved the world, that He gave His only begotten Son, that whosoever believes in Him should not perish, but have eternal life" (John 3:16).

I'm so thankful that "whosoever" includes me, it includes you, and it includes Gina, who so many years ago sang:

At my worst You found me
  At my worst You died
At my worst You loved me
  And at my worst You tried
To tell me that the best thing I could do
  Would be to give my life to You
At my worst You loved me
  And now I love You too.

"Therefore if any man is in Christ, he is a new creature; the old things passed away; behold, new things have come" (2 Corinthians 5:17).

SONG INDEX

SONG	ALBUM	YEAR
Here We Are	Tell 'Em Again	1978
I've Never Seen The Righteous Forsaken	All That Matters	1979
I Have Hope	Completely Taken In	1993
Mount Up With Wings	Beyond the Curtain	1988
This Too Shall Pass	Face of Mercy	1995
Worth The Waiting	I Saw the Lord	1981
Heal Me	Beyond the Curtain	1988
If All I Ever Knew	All That Matters	1979
He'll Dry the Tears	Against the Wind	1986
He Knew Me Then	Just Right	1976
Through the Flame	Through the Flame	1990
Waiting	Against the Wind	1986
Before Your Throne	Before Your Throne	1999
Strength	Face of Mercy	1995
The Good Samaritan	Just the Way I Feel It	1971
Rise Again	Dallas Holm & Praise Live	1977
At My Worst	Tell 'Em Again	1978

** *Album title and date on which songs first appeared*

Lyric sheets available at www.dallasholm.com/lyrics